ADOLPHE MONOD'S FAREWELL

ADOLPHE MONOD'S FAREWELL

to his friends and to his church

★

A new translation by
THE REV. OWEN THOMAS, B.A.

For I am now ready to be offered, and the time of my departure is at hand. I have fought a good fight, I have finished my course, I have kept the faith.
2. Tim 4. 6, 7

THE BANNER OF TRUTH TRUST
78b Chiltern Street, London, W.1.

First published in French 1874
First Banner of Truth Trust edition 1962

Set in 11 point Baskerville and printed in Great Britain
by Billing and Sons Limited Guildford & London

CONTENTS

BIOGRAPHICAL INTRODUCTION

WHEN in September, 1855, Adolphe Monod was overtaken by a fatal illness it seemed that the earthly ministry of the foremost preacher in France had come to an end. His voice would no more rouse the thronged congregations in the Oratoire, Paris, as it had done for nine years past, and soon his life would no more be the "lighthouse," as a contemporary described him, "to whom everyone looked as the sailor in the storm." Thus suddenly reduced to the pain of a sick-bed at the age of fifty-three, Monod had but one concern: "O my God," he prayed, "is my work finished? Thou only knowest . . . *I should so much have wished to leave behind me some lasting monument for Thy glory.*" His prayer was answered, yet not in the way that he might have imagined. God did not restore him to his former work but brought him to exercise a new ministry—the ministry of suffering and patience which occasioned the contents of this book. As long as evangelical literature is read, *Adolphe Monod's Farewell* will be remembered as the most enduring monument he left to the glory of God.

Born on January 21st, 1802, Monod was the fourth son of Jean Monod, the Swiss pastor of the French church at Copenhagen, and, after 1808, of the Reformed Church in Paris. Adolphe was educated at the Collège Bonaparte in Paris, and after the completion of his studies there he followed his elder brother to Geneva to study theology. A great change had taken place amongst the students at Geneva shortly before Monod's arrival. In the middle of November, 1816, an unknown Scotsman, Robert Haldane, had arrived in Geneva and with no means but prayer and faith in the power of Scripture he had boldly attacked the prevailing heresies which had long dishonoured Calvin's city. Adolphe's elder brother Frederic (1794-1863) describes the state of things among the students prior to the memorable winter of 1816: "Though students of theology, true theology was one of the things of which we knew the least. God's Holy Word was to us *terra ignota,* whilst Unitarianism, with all its chilling influence and all its soul-destroying appendages, was the only doctrine taught to us by our Professors." In such circumstances the word quickly spread that a man had arrived "who knows the Bible like Calvin!" Frederic Monod was soon converted and became one of Haldane's interpreters. In a hotel room—described by J. H. Merle d'Aubigné as "the birthplace of the Second Reformation in Geneva"—the message of the Epistle to the Romans poured light into the minds of the gathered students. "I see now that doctrine in the Bible," exclaimed Merle d'Aubigné, after an exposition of man's corrupt nature. "Yes," replied Haldane, "but do you see it in your heart?"

Through these events there commenced a wide-spread revival of the gospel in Europe and while Adolphe was not himself converted by these means there can be no doubt that his days at Geneva were in measure a preparation for what was soon to follow.

Monod graduated from Geneva in 1824, and the following year, after a visit to England, he set out with his brother Guillaume on a tour of Italy. His impression of these two countries was vastly different: "How happy is a Protestant minister who labours in a Protestant country!" he wrote to his mother after witnessing crowded English churches. In Naples, on the other hand, he found the French-speaking Protestants without any means of public worship and in response to their appeal Monod undertook the difficult charge of being their first pastor. His eighteen months in Naples was a time of trial but it was the turning-point of his life, for when he returned to France in 1827 he was resting fully on the great facts of the gospel and ready to devote all his energies to the service of Christ.

Monod's subsequent ministry may be divided into three more or less equal periods—approximately ten years at Lyons, at Montauban and at Paris. He became the minister of the Reformed Church at Lyons in December, 1827, and before long his evangelical preaching aroused such opposition that pressure was put on the Government to have him deposed. When he was finally put out of the National Church in 1832 a number of like-minded Christians came out with him and formed the Evangelical Church of Lyons with Monod as their first pastor. About the same time Monod received several invitations to accept a professorship but he would not leave this young church until it was well established. Four years later when he did respond to a call to the Chair of Moral Theology at Montauban, the church at Lyons had made such progress that two pastors and two laymen were required to continue the work. Besides fulfilling his duties as a Professor at Montauban, Monod preached regularly in the town and in the college chapel and never forgot that his chief aim as a minister of Christ was to save men from destruction. His long academic vacations enabled him to make extensive preaching tours especially in the South of France and wherever he appeared multitudes followed him, attracted by the spiritual power of his preaching and the fervour of his delivery.

By the time Monod was called to the Reformed Church in Paris in 1847, his name was everywhere known. "He was," declared Professor de Félice, "twice over the first of the Protestant preachers of France, first for the excellency of his oratorical genius, and then for the holiness of his life." Despite the extent of his labours—he sometimes preached four times on a Sunday—Monod remained a constant student of the Scriptures which he read daily in the original. He was a man of prayer. He visited the poor and the sick, instructed his own family, and until 1852 when his health began to decline, he continued his preaching tours sometimes as far afield as Scotland which he visited in 1849.

The termination of such a ministry was a sore loss to France, yet with his opportunities for spiritual usefulness suddenly reduced to the dimensions of a single bedroom, Monod devoted the months that remained to the ministry that abides in the pages of this book. Commencing on October 14th, 1855, he began to partake the Lord's Supper with a varying company of friends who gathered in his room every Sunday afternoon. Too weak to speak for long and too ill to prepare anything more than a short meditation, Monod used these occasions to commend the Saviour who now sustained him amidst incessant suffering. Knowing the time was short, his light shone brighter—no longer as an eloquent preacher but as a suffering saint nearing his end—and if the radiance of things eternal falls on the reader as he goes through the following chapters it is because the author was daily entering into deeper communion with Him who has brought "immortality and life to light."

These pages were neither written nor corrected* by Monod; but they are the words of his short discourses taken down carefully as he spoke and purposely left in their original spontaneous form. Consequently it is not surprising if these simple addresses do not convey an idea of the pure style that characterized the author's published sermons, but such subjects and such an occasion can well stand without the finish that we expect from more normal works. By their literary form as well as by their peculiar unction and power, we are thus reminded that Monod literally spoke as a *dying man* to dying men.

The delivery of these exhortations continued for nearly six months though they were often the means of aggravating his physical sufferings. Like Edward Payson who on his death bed saw the privilege of being a minister of the gospel in a new light, Monod declared, "If every week I

* With the exception of the discourse entitled *The Scriptures*.

must obtain by redoubled sufferings the privilege of announcing Thy Word, may Thy will and not mine be done . . . It is a sacrifice I willingly offer to God." On November 25, 1855, he said to his friends, "I suffered much this morning, and it was to be feared that I should not be able to speak this afternoon; but God suspended my sufferings for an hour, to allow me to glorify Him; and He granted me the favour of exercising this little ministry, which is so great a consolation for me." And again on March 2, 1856, a month before his death, he said, "Another Sunday in which God has allowed me to address a few words to our little assembly, notwithstanding my increasing weakness, to which my feeble voice bore testimony. May He deign to support me to the end, and grant me the grace, if it be possible (for I wish not to dictate to Him), to cease to proclaim His Name only when I cease to live." On March 23 he gave his last address on *The Resurrection of Christ*—though in such weakness that he seemed ready to faint in pronouncing the closing words. The following Sunday, March 30, "scarcely knowing whether he should be able to make himself heard, he collected the little strength he had to glorify the everlasting and infinite love of God," and terminated with a prayer of thanksgiving his ministry upon earth. Before the sun had set on the following Lord's Day, April 6, 1856, Monod had entered "the land of pure delight where saints immortal reign."

"More than anyone else," wrote Professor de Félice in his *History of the French Protestants,* "Adolphe Monod recalled to us the venerable image of the Christians of the primitive Church." That such a man, who spent the last twenty-five years of his life in whole-hearted devotion to Christ, found it necessary to speak so fully as he does in this book on *A Dying Man's Regrets,* is a sobering fact. Life in retrospect, under the shadow of a coming eternity, and weighed in the balances of Scripture, is an experience which all who read this book will one day share. Our present view-point will soon be changed—things that are temporal must give way to things eternal—and to realise these facts in advance is to heed the exhortation of the Apostle, "Abide in him; that, when he shall appear, we may have confidence, and not be ashamed before him at his coming." (1 John 2 : 28).

Iain Murray
August 1962

I

EVERYTHING IN SCRIPTURE IS IDEAL

[14 October 1855]

My dear friends, brothers and sisters beloved, with whom I am so happy to receive the flesh and blood of our Saviour—that flesh which is "food indeed" and that blood which is "drink indeed" for those who receive them with faith, by the power of the Holy Spirit—there is in the Scripture a clear mark which would suffice by itself to make one recognise it as the Word of God. It is that everything in it is absolute and perfect. The Scripture does not dream of calling us only to a certain degree of holiness, by a certain measure of faith: for all idea of measure is contrary to the instinct of the Bible, because it is contrary to the nature of God. The Scriptural ideal is not like that of the poets. They take the things of earth and lift them up to the third heaven. The Bible does the very opposite: it takes the invisible only as reality and the visible simply as the shadow of real things. It considers all things from God's point of view. I was struck by this thought only this morning, as I meditated before the Lord on what I might say to you on the subject of the Communion and the cross of Jesus Christ, through which alone we find remission of our sins.

In the Bible we are presented everywhere with *sin* in its *true sense*. Not one of us could conjure up an idea of sin in all its horrible criminality, as God sees it. We are inhabitants of a world which drinks iniquity like water and eats it like bread, and we live in an atmosphere so saturated with it, that we are no longer conscious of the sin which completely envelops us everywhere. Let me tell you briefly my own experience. We find written in the Bible these words (Titus 3.3): "For we ourselves also were sometimes foolish, disobedient, deceived, serving divers lusts and pleasures, living in malice and envy, hateful, and hating one another."

For a long time it was impossible for me to accept this statement, which seemed to me to be quite manifestly an exaggeration. I confess that even after God by His grace had inclined my heart towards Him on the day which He had marked out from all eternity, I remained for a long time still unable to accept it fully. Moreover, I confess that even now, long afterwards, I cannot comprehend the fulness of its meaning—not that I am any longer unconvinced that it is absolutely and entirely true, and that if I do not realise it in my own experience, the fault is entirely mine. It is for this very reason that I have come to realise the necessity of having a testimony, outside of ourselves, existing before us and beyond us. Accordingly, I accept this statement in Titus as coming from God Himself, because I find it written in His Word, and my prayer is that He would reveal the full meaning of it to me by His Spirit. I have consequently, by His grace, come to see this doctrine more clearly, and to feel the truth of it more and more in my heart, not just as one year has succeeded another—these things do not come as quickly as that—but over a period of several years. Furthermore, I am sure that when this veil of flesh is laid aside I shall recognise that this passage of Scripture was the most faithful and lifelike portrait of my heart that could ever be painted—I mean my natural heart. Let us ask God to reveal to us our sinful state; but let us not be impatient, because He knows very well that if He makes the realisation of our sin develop more quickly than the realisation of His mercy, then we would fall into despair.

But *forgiveness* is also presented to us everywhere in the Scripture in its *true sense*. If only part of our sins were forgiven; if, say, out of a thousand or a million sins (if they can be counted!) there remained just one unpardoned, this forgiveness would be no use to us at all. But, on the contrary, it is *full* pardon. The passage quoted just now (2 Cor. 5:21): "For he hath made him to be sin for us, who knew no sin; that we might be made the righteousness of God in him.") is one of my favourite passages of Scripture. Jesus Christ has not just atoned for some sins: He has atoned for *sin*. He was not considered a sinner. He was made *sin* itself, and, mystery of mysteries, all the wrath of God gathered upon that holy innocent head. Likewise we are not only regarded as righteous in Him, but as *righteousness* itself; so that, when God looks on us in Jesus Christ, He sees us as His beloved Son Himself and finds in us all that can draw out His complacent love. We who believe have been given to Jesus Christ by God, as the reward of His sacrifice. He can no more fail in His promise to us than in that to Jesus Christ Himself; indeed in the matter of our salvation all His perfections are so involved that this gift of infinite mercy becomes, as it were, a right merited by our perfect righteousness in Jesus Christ. The very terms which the Bible uses in showing us what sin is in the sight of God also show how effectively He has dealt with our sins. He has "cast them behind His back," as if He was afraid to see them again. They are "cast into the depth of the sea, blotted out as a thick cloud"; by this we see what is meant for God to forget. The Lord is represented as taking deliberate steps to forget; not that He is forgetful, but rather that He deliberately and completely wipes out the very memory of them.

Finally the Scripture, when speaking of sanctification, speaks of it in its *true sense*. In and of ourselves we can have no idea of what the Scripture demands of us, of the degree of holiness to which we can and ought to attain. What a fulness there is in these words (1 Thess. 5:23): "And the very God of peace sanctify you wholly; and I pray God your whole spirit and soul and body be preserved blameless unto the coming of our Lord Jesus Christ." And to prove to us that it is not simply a wish, the apostle adds immediately afterwards: "Faithful is he that calleth you, who also will do it." He cannot possibly refuse this blessing, because He cannot break His word. It is inconceivable. But how may we arrive at this holiness? How indeed did the holy men of God, whom the Bible holds up to us as examples, attain to greatness? It was not by their own light, nor by their natural gifts, but by their faith. Take for instance St. James: to illustrate the power of faith and prayer he takes perhaps the most miraculous man in the Bible, in his most miraculous miracle. He points to the boldness of that prayer of Elijah as quite a simple matter, and offers him as an example to the least and humblest of us, in order to show what the persevering (or literally *energumen*) prayer of a righteous man can do.

If, from today, each one of us could feel in our hearts the enormity of our sin, the fulness of its pardon and the power of holiness to which we ought to attain, what a change would take place in our lives and what a salutary influence it would have upon the Church itself!

II

HAPPY IN LIFE AND DEATH

[21 October 1855]

Philippians 1 : 19-26

MY dear friends, I want to draw your attention to the way in which the apostle Paul regards life and death in this passage. Notice part of this statement which serves as a point of departure, and is as it were the motto of his Christian life: "For me to live is Christ, and to die is gain." In other words, my life, my natural life, which I enjoy today and from which I may pass away tomorrow, has no other employment but that of following and serving Jesus Christ. "To die is gain": this statement needs no explanation. Before that, the apostle wonders which is better for him, to live or to die. This question has often come before us, and perhaps we have answered like the apostle. But it is to be feared that we meant it in quite a different way. If we preferred death, then it meant, "I do not know which I should dread the most, the afflictions of life from which death would deliver me, or the terrors of death from which life preserves me." We mean that life and death appear to us as two evils, and we do not know which of them is the lesser evil. As for the apostle, they both appear to him as two immense blessings and he does not know which is the better of them!

Personally he prefers to die, to be with Christ. As far as the Church and the world are concerned he prefers to live, in order to serve Jesus Christ, extend His kingdom and win souls to Him. What a splendid attitude to life and death, splendid because it is dominated and sanctified entirely by love, and identical with the attitude of Jesus Christ Himself! Let us try to enter into this sentiment. Life is good; death is good. Death is good because it frees us from the miseries of this life, above all because even if our life were filled with all the joy that earth can give, death gives us entrance into a joy and a glory of which we can have little idea now. We therefore must look upon death as being a thing desirable in itself. Let us not avoid those things which may remind us of it. Let all the illnesses, all the sudden deaths, all that takes place around us, remind us that for each one of us death can come at any moment. Life is also good, because we can serve Jesus Christ, glorify Jesus Christ, imitate Jesus Christ. It is not worth living for anything else. All that we have of strength, breath, life and faculties must be consecrated, devoted, sanctified and sacrificed for the service of our Saviour Jesus Christ. This crucified life of sacrifice is the happy life, even in the midst of the bitterest mortal sufferings; because in it we can taste for ourselves and spread all around us the most precious blessings.

Let us love life and appreciate well its value, but only to fill it with Jesus Christ. We can only have such an outlook as the Holy Spirit transforms us into new men. But do let us give attention to this fact: it is not just our own spirit which must be upheld, consoled and strengthened. It is the Spirit of God who must come and dwell in us. We often try to work upon ourselves to cultivate our own spirit; that is all to the good; but it is not enough. We must have more. Jesus Christ Himself must dwell in our hearts by His Holy Spirit.

Only, friends! consider what are the promises of the Gospel, and we will see how far we are from possessing them and enjoying them. May God be pleased to open the heavens above our heads, and reveal them all to us and fill us with all wisdom, and make us see that, even down here, we can attain perfect joy as we wait in expectation for the full realisation of felicity and victory to come. May He lead us to gather all the blessings that Heaven is pleased to pour out upon the earth which opens to receive it, so that we may come to know that, though the world can smite us low and trouble us, it cannot extinguish the faithfulness of God nor annul His promises, nor cast a veil, not even the slightest cloud, over the love with which God has loved us in Jesus Christ.

III

FREQUENT COMMUNION

[28 October 1855]

MY dear friends, I want you to know that I have found much sweetness, and I hope much fruit, during my illness, in taking the Communion frequently.

It is a great evil that the Communion is celebrated so rarely in our Church, and attempts are being made everywhere to remedy it. Our Reformers in establishing this order of things took care to explain that they were only doing it for a time in order to prevent the very grave abuses which had crept into the primitive Church.

But what they did for a time has remained for centuries in most of our Churches. Now at last we are entering upon the time when frequent Communion will be given back to us. Calvin says in one place that Communion should be celebrated at least every Sunday. Notice that "*at least*". If every Sunday is "at least," then what is "at most?" According to Calvin, "at most" is to take it like the early Christians did, as we see clearly in Acts, *every day,* and from house to house, following the family meal.

Each one of you has surely noticed that the rare observance of Communion has given rise to I do not know what strange and extraordinary ideas of the Communion, because of the preparations which must precede it and the emotions which follow.

One can be excused for thinking that it is the rareness of the Communion which has given rise to most of the controversies on the subject. On the other hand, frequent Communion makes the true character of the sacrament much more clearly understood, and daily Communion can only make it more so. It teaches one to relate the Communion to all that is most simple in the Christian life, as a meal relates to all that is most simple in ordinary life.

At any rate, it is in seeing the Communion as the simplest expression of our faith that we profit most from it and draw from it the most fruit. Then it will feed our soul with the flesh and blood of Jesus Christ.

There is in our Confession of Faith a passage on this subject so beautiful that I will read it to you. It expresses what I would like to say myself:-

"We confess that the Lord's Supper is a testimony to us of the union which we have with Jesus Christ, inasmuch as He was not only once dead and raised from the dead for us, but also feeds us and nourishes us truly with His flesh and His blood, so that we are one with Him and His life is communicated to us. Now, although He be in Heaven until He comes to judge all men, nevertheless, we believe that by the secret incomprehensible virtue of His Spirit He nourishes and sustains us with the substance of His body and blood. This we hold indeed to take place spiritually, not to substitute in place of fact and truth what is merely imagined or thought, but inasmuch as this mystery surpasses in its loftiness the measure of our senses and all the order of nature. We believe that, as in the Lord's Supper so in Baptism, God actually and really gives us what is symbolised therein. And consequently we link to the signs the true possession and enjoyment of that which is there presented to us. And so all who bring to Christ's holy table a pure faith, like an empty vessel, really receive that to which the signs give testimony: that is, that the body and blood of Jesus Christ serve no less as meat and drink to the soul than bread and wine are to the body.

"The bread and wine given to us in the Lord's Supper serve as true spiritual food to us, in so far as they show, as it were by visible demonstration, the flesh of Jesus Christ to be our meat, and His blood our drink."

I will add just this to this admirable quotation: one

day Pastor Vernay read these very words to a few Lutheran friends who were discussing the Communion with him. After he had finished, his friends said to him, "That expresses exactly what we believe." To which Mr. Vernay replied, "These words were taken from the Confession of Faith of the Reformed Churches." Which goes to prove that in holding closely to the Scriptures, as is done in this quotation, one rises by faith and love above the field of controversy!

Well, my friends, what we testify to in the Communion, which we have just celebrated, is that the body and blood of the Saviour are truly food and drink; I say that the highest Christian ambition is to feed ourselves upon them day and night, and to seek all our strength in a real, profound and living fellowship with Jesus Christ alone. It is by prayer that we maintain this fellowship with Jesus Christ, which will make us able to do what He did and to be what He was; but it is the prayer of faith, earnest and persevering, which accepts no refusal, demands all that the Father has promised us in His Word, and will not be silent. Prayer that keeps us on our knees pressing on even through blood and tears, until we obtain what we ask. Oh! what power we could have, what joy, unchangeable and independent of all our sufferings in this miserable body, alreadv perhaps wasted and half-destroyed, but which is even now the temple of the Holy Spirit, and tomorrow will go to be transformed into a glorious spiritual body, that is to say, entirely filled with the Holy Spirit, like the body of Jesus Christ Himself. What joy we could have! I do not say if we had the means, because we *have* got the means; but if we used the means which we have got, always to overcome the pains and struggles of the flesh and to reach the heart of our Father, the joy of our Saviour, and the power of the Holy Spirit.

Meditate, I solemnly ask you, on the Holy Spirit. Read and re-read the discourses of Jesus Christ in the last chapters of St. John's Gospel, the eighth chapter of Romans and other passages, to learn what mighty power and consolation we have in the Holy Spirit, who is none other than God Himself. Yes, my God, none other than Thyself, coming to dwell in the body of Thy poor child, a miserable sinner, maimed by suffering and sin, but saved by grace and washed in the blood of the spotless Lamb of God!

Why, when we have such promises, should we let ourselves stop halfway? Why should we moan about our hunger and thirst, when we have before us a table with abundant provision, to which we need only stretch out the hand of faith to feed ourselves until we are fully satisfied, and have life more abundant?

Ah! if only this little handful of Christians gathered here could resolve to have the full joy of salvation, to pray perseveringly,* like Elijah; if only they could resolve to conquer their natural slackness, their spiritual sluggishness, their unbelief! What could we not do, if we went through the world like the twelve apostles? We would arouse all Paris; we would draw after us all our brothers and sisters whose hearts would be touched by seeing the Gospel realised in our lives!

My God, herein lies our deepest misery, that having such promises we do so little. Come and help us, and grant that this little fellowship of the upper room may be for all those who have taken part in it or who have been present, the beginning of a new Christian life, whether in life or death, and that we may be so conformed to Jesus Christ that we live as He lived, and as He said "He that hath seen me hath seen the Father," we also may be able to say: "He who has seen me has seen my Master."

Pour out this blessing on these friends who have come to comfort me in my affliction, my *happy affliction*!

* Literally " to pray in praying."

IV

THE PASTOR SUFFERING FOR THE GOOD OF THE CHURCH

[4 November 1855]

HOW gracious God is in giving us the Communion, such a simple and at the same time such a profound image of the invisible grace of the Lord!

The whole foundation of the Gospel is in that table, if we meditate on the teaching which Scripture gives upon it. For we find two things in it, first, Jesus Christ as the one who was dying for us; that death, that blood, that atoning sacrifice, the only hope of our salvation, accomplishing absolutely everything for the elect of God. Then again we see in it the same Jesus who died, entering our hearts and feeding us, imparting life to us by His flesh and His blood, and thereby making us partakers of His nature, as He Himself partakes of the Father's nature.

To die to ourselves and to live for Jesus Christ by the Holy Spirit as a consequence of His death for us on the cross, that is the whole Gospel, the whole faith, the whole Christian life.

I want further to add a few words, which Paul said: "Let no one faint because of the sufferings which I endure." But I do not claim to be able to say them as he did. Certainly it is not for me to compare Paul's great afflictions endured directly for the service of God with those which God has done the favour of visiting upon me. But I desire to make of them an affliction endured for the sake of the Gospel, and therefore in my own little measure for you, by the spirit in which I accept them.

I wish no one to be dismayed by them. Perhaps some of my good friends are troubled by the thought of the evils which I suffer. Well, do not be troubled. Give me a mark of brotherly love by not being troubled, but stimulated and revived by them in a healthy way. It is not that I do not suffer or that I suffer without feeling. I am not a Stoic; by the grace of God I am a Christian, and I am not ashamed to say that there are moments when I cry with tears more than I pray: I recall that my Saviour gave vent to " strong crying with tears." But although these things are painful to the flesh, they are attended by such great blessings that the feeling of thankfulness must prevail in my heart—and in yours. How blessed I am, my dear friends, that God, wishing to use one of us to remind the others of lessons concerning life, thoughts about death, sin, grace and sanctification, should choose me!

What a privilege, that in taking me He has spared my brothers, and what a privilege that He has chosen me to give you these lessons on everlasting life! Then think how fitting it all is to make me appreciate a Christian death, at whatever moment it should fall to me. Let us all seek only to glorify God. If He is pleased to heal me, I ask that it shall be for His glory; if He is pleased to take me, I shall be happy to be gathered into His bosom. I cannot tell which would be best for me or for the Church. I abandon myself completely to Him. But what a gracious preferment it is for me to be thus ripened by suffering! You therefore have cause to rejoice for me; and for yourselves, because is it not true that my affliction has helped to make you think about death, eternity and the truths of the Gospel? Is it not true that by the brotherly love which unites us you have been driven to prayer? I feel borne up on the prayers of the people of God and I am filled with joy and thankfulness.

Well, is not that wonderful for you? Do you not feel that all that is happening to me is calculated to spread among my intimate friends, and particularly in my family, a spirit of peace and serenity; and that our house is, in a measure less imperfect than it has been until now, a house of prayer, where the name of God is constantly being invoked, because it has been constantly invoked by others upon it?

These then are blessings to be reaped. And do understand what sweetness I derive from this thought that I am afflicted for your benefit; because nothing can bring my sufferings nearer to those of my Saviour. So I say in the spirit of the same St. Paul whom I have already quoted: "Therefore I rejoice in my sufferings for you, and I fill up in my flesh what is lacking of the afflictions of Christ for His body, which is the Church."

O wonder of the grace of God! O power of the Gospel! O bitterness of sin! But O, immovable firmness of grace! Let us fight against sin, my friends: it is the only evil, the *only* evil.

And now, when I find myself in the presence of sin, called upon to review before God all the sins of my life and to ask Him to forgive them, it is now that I feel how terrible the struggle is, how deeply rooted sin is, and how foolish it is to complain to God for the evils which He sends us, since those very evils are not sufficient to root out that accursed pride, that frightful selfishness, and above all that detestable unbelief.

May the peace of God be with you. Set personal feelings aside. Do not see in me the father, the friend—or at least only in a certain measure, but see in me before all else the minister of Jesus Christ, and ask God that I may be kept faithful in this ministry until my very last breath.

Do not look at the man in me, but look at the work which God will accomplish in me—and in you. Let us take courage. Let us ask God to fill us with His Spirit, to make us able to govern the flesh by the spirit until He takes us from the evil to come, and to grant us through Jesus Christ to taste in a glorified body and a sanctified soul, all the joy, the bliss and the glory which the shed blood of Jesus Christ alone has merited for us!

V

ON READING THE BIBLE

[11 November 1855]

IT is my custom in my present circumstances to address a few words of Christian exhortation to the friends who are so kind as to meet around my bed. Today my state of suffering prevents me from having this consolation. I am inclined to recount to you a fact of Christian experience which may lead you to a helpful reflection on the Word of God. I shall take it quite simply as it came to me in what happened this week.

During one of my nights of much suffering and little sleep, about half past four in the morning, I had settled down in my bed hoping to get some sleep. I asked my companion*—one of those good young people who kindly dedicate part of their strength to me—to read a chapter of the Word of God to me. He suggested reading the eighth chapter of Romans. I agreed, but asked him to go back to the sixth or even the fifth chapter to catch the sequence of ideas. We read straight off, those four chapters five, six, seven, eight, and I could no longer ever think of sleeping, so much was my attention, my interest, my admiration arrested by the heavenly language of St. Paul, or rather I should say the Holy Spirit speaking through St. Paul. Then we read the following chapters right to the end, still with sustained, consistent interest. Then we read the first four chapters so that we should not lose anything, and thus read

* Adolphe Monod had someone to sit up with him every night during more than six months from a small group of young friends, nearly all medical students. Their devotion and affectionate care sweetened for him the long hours of sleeplessness and suffering.

the entire epistle. About two hours had gone by in this reading, and I was thinking of nothing save hearing the Word of God and profiting by it: and the Lord in His goodness compensated me for the sleep which I had lost. But I could not tell you how much I was struck in this reading of the Epistle to the Romans in its entirety by a hidden store of divinity, truth, holiness, love and power which is laid up, imprinted on every page and in every word. My young friend and I felt, without at first sharing our thoughts, that we were listening to a voice from Heaven; and that, independently of all the testimony which witnesses to the divine inspiration and authority of the Scripture, it gave its own full and sufficient testimony to itself, as Jesus did to Himself, by His works. We felt also how useful it is to read the Scripture as a whole, and how much one loses in only taking from it detached portions, fragments or verses. You cannot understand a book without from time to time reading it as a whole.

Two methods of studying the Word of God are hereby implied: one, studying it as a whole, to produce the impression so full of blessing which we had just received: the other, studying it in detail to take due note of every verse and every word. But the principal impression was one of humiliation. We said one to another: What! we have such a treasure store as this near at hand, and we neglect to dip into it. We had just spent two hours in Heaven and found ourselves transported not only into the company of the best of men, the privileged, inspired instruments of the Holy Spirit, but also of the elect angels, and in the fellowship of Jesus Christ. Therefore, placing this resolution in the care of Him who alone can safeguard the resolutions of His children, we determined to give ourselves, with an entirely new ardour, to the study of the Scripture; to sacrifice if necessary the reading of a whole pile of books which, while quite useful and instructive, do not compare with the Word of God; and to live with His Word as we wish to live with God Himself, because reading His Word, inspired by the

Spirit of God, is like holding a conversation with God. I do commend to you, my dear friends, the Word of God for your constant study and deep meditation. It will make us stand out above all others; it will be the strength of our life, the joy of our heart, and our strong consolation in life and in death through Jesus Christ. I ask this for you, as for myself. Amen.

VI

GOD GLORIFIED IN SUFFERING

[18 November 1855]

THE prayer of our brother which we have just heard was full of this thought: that we must each one of us according to his position glorify God. I want in a few words to make you, and also myself, feel what an immense privilege it is to be called to glorify God. Just think what it means! God, the Sovereign Creator, the unique Author of all things, by whose only will all things subsist and have been created; God, the Saviour of a lost and guilty humanity, the only Consoler of a suffering humanity, God, from whom all good proceeds, who does not need us, invites us to add something to His glory by giving testimony to Him before His creatures, thus contributing in our own way to the hallowing of His Name! He desires that to be the supreme law of our life.

True piety, as well as true wisdom and true philosophy, even though human, demands a single principle which will direct the whole of life and to which we may relate everything. And this unity, which men go out to seek, some in the world, others in themselves, or in some imaginary god, we ourselves find in the living and true God who alone is holy, wise and eternal, on whom alone depends both our eternal happiness in its full development and also the least blessing which we can enjoy day by day, in the feelings of our heart, or even in the sensations of our poor bodies!

And who are those whom He has called to contribute to His glory? There are of course the angels, and they are indeed happy to do it, thinking what a great privilege it is for them. But not only the angels, there remain also we miserable sinners, worthy of the wrath of God, placed by our works under His curse, whom He not only pulls out of this deep abyss with His hand, but to whom He says, as He pulls us out, "Now, glorify Me"; as if we could possibly give anything to Him from whom we have received all things, beginning with the forgiveness of our sins! Oh! if only we could feel what grace God shows us in employing us to add something to His glory, we should not be occupied with anything else and we should find in that, my beloved, our sweetest and deepest consolation. For it is not only pardoned sinners who are called to glorify God after having been saved, but also suffering miserable sinners, whose lives are sore beset with sufferings of the soul as well as the body. These would seem to be excluded from the privilege of glorifying God, absorbed as they are by the pains and tribulations of life. Ah! but not at all! They are the very ones who are specially called to glorify Him, and who find in their sufferings, as in their sins which have been expiated, a means of giving more glory to Him who has taught us to say, "When I am weak, then I am strong." What consolation for those who suffer, to be able to say: I can by my sufferings, which I bear patiently and peaceably until such time as I can do so joyously and gloriously: I can, by these very sufferings render to God a glory which I would not be able to render otherwise; and what infinite sweetness those who suffer find in this thought!

It is this that makes suffering a privilege. For a Christian, suffering is a privilege. To suffer much is a special privilege. And all those who suffer must enter into my thought and "commit their souls to God, as to a faithful Creator, in well doing." Alas! we cannot do it of ourselves. "The spirit is willing, but the flesh is weak," and the moment we are lifted up to heaven by the simple words of the Gospel, then we are taken as it were by the heels, by that miserable flesh which drags and pulls us down towards the earth and binds us by the weight of our sufferings. My friends, this is our lifelong battle, it is our battle in life and in death.

But with us we have Jesus, the author and perfecter of our faith, who was Himself consecrated by suffering and who also is able to succour those who are tempted. Our constant prayer should be:

"Lord, increase our faith! Lord, I believe; help thou mine unbelief."

O my friends, you who in your brotherly love have come to unite with me in celebrating this sweet Communion—which is such a vivid image to us of our communion with God and with one another—may God bless each one of you, and give each one of us grace to live only for His glory, to suffer only for His glory, to speak only for His glory, and to expect even to die for His glory, through Jesus Christ crucified and risen from the dead!

VII

THE LOVE OF GOD MANIFESTED IN HIS PEOPLE

[25 November 1855]

MY dear friends, I feared that I would not be able to address you today, owing to extreme suffering and fatigue; however, once again the Lord has graciously given me some relief. You cannot imagine how thankful I am for having the faculty, against all human expectation, of thus exercising every Sunday in some measure this ministry which I should like to continue until my last breath.

For my ministry is my life, and I feel that when I have no ministry to exercise I shall be taken home to exercise another and better ministry. And ask God that He will not take away from me this consolation of being able thus to receive the body and blood of my Saviour every Sunday to strengthen both my body and my soul in Him; and also to address a few words of edification and exhortation to my brethren.

Last Sunday I emphasised in a few words to the friends who were present (and who change each Sunday) the immense privilege of being able to glorify God, which we are not simply permitted, but commanded to do. Today I will add that there is a point of view from which we are especially obliged and especially blessed in being able to glorify Him.

If among the perfections of God which we are called upon to show before men there was a perfection whose manifestation was particularly pleasing to Him, would it not be true that by reproducing and manifesting that perfection we could glorify Him the best? Very well then, what is that perfection in which God best manifests His presence?

Is it not goodness? It is written, is it not, that God is love Now God is just and yet it is not written "God is justice." God is powerful but it is not written "God is power." Ther are however two perfections to which this honour is paic by the beloved disciple who lay on the bosom of th Saviour—holiness and love: "God is light, God is love" and whereas he says once in his first epistle "God is light," he says twice within a few verses, "God is love," as if to lif this perfection above the other. If this is so, my dear friends then what we must do to glorify God is to manifest that lov which is in Him in such a way that in seeing how we live how we speak, how we act, how we suffer, live and die, me may not admire us but admire the love of God in us.

And how can we manifest the love of God? Jesus Chris is the example. He above all manifested that love: H glorified God among all men, and tenderly constrained al who beheld Him with faith to say as they saw Him: "Wha love there is in God," since the one who said "He that hat seen me hath seen the Father" is Himself so much fille with love. And how did He show it? He showed it i everything. But above all He showed it in suffering for Hi brethren, first of all for their temporal deliverance: "H went about doing good." But these healings were only type and image of the true spiritual deliverance, and Hi sufferings were above all for that.

And that is the highest point which we reach in mani festing the love of God: to suffer for our brethren, an especially for the salvation of their souls. We can all do it my dear friends. Not perhaps in the same special an direct way as the apostle Paul, whose entire life was conse crated to the preaching of the Gospel, and who said: "I fil up in my flesh that which is behind of the sufferings o Christ for his body's sake, which is the church"—there i no need to seek an exact interpretation of these words; ther is an infinity of charity and profundity of love in thes words of St. Paul which cannot be confined to merel human definitions. His whole life was filled with a compul sion to imitate his Saviour, who "left us an example that we should follow his steps," and as his Saviour suffered to save men, Paul felt compelled to suffer for his brethren —not to save them (for no one has declared more clearly that no man, or creature, can do anything to save us), but to labour for their salvation: "For in so doing thou shalt both save thyself and those who hear thee." But even though we may not have to endure such sufferings as Paul endured directly for the service of God and the good of men, yet all of our sufferings can be made to take on that character by the spirit which we bring to them.

If in "suffering by the will of God we commit our souls to him as to a faithful Creator in well doing," and if we endeavour to turn all the sufferings which God shall be pleased to send us, of soul, spirit and body, to the temporal and above all spiritual good of men, we shall have attained the purpose for which God sent them to us. And generally speaking, my beloved, the more we love, the more we walk in that spiritual communion with God and one another, the more we shall become like Him. Let us therefore go into the world, each one of us, and be like a reflection of the divine love. May all our words, our works, our most secret thoughts and most intimate prayers, breathe that love which God has revealed to us in Jesus Christ and compel men to say: "Oh, how true it is! God is love."

VIII

FAITH

[2 December 1855]

Hebrews 10 : 32-39

THAT faith which is the subject of the verses which w began by reading and which is the subject of th admirable eleventh chapter of Hebrews, which follows c immediately afterwards—that faith of which the sacrame of the Lord's Supper is so simple and so profound an imag that faith, my friends, is our only power, and our only peac For faith is nothing less than the power of God placed the disposal of man. In this eleventh chapter Paul compr hends in faith all the gifts, not only sanctification, but al prophecy, and miracles. He does not say that Mos crossed the Red Sea because he was clothed with supe natural power, but he says it was because he *believe* Neither does he say that Abraham did all the wonderf things that he did by supernatural power, but because l *believed*. Hence we must admire not only that the Ho Spirit explains all the great works of the saints entirely l an inner spiritual principle, but further by a principle whic is accessible to us all. For after all, if nothing is mentione but faith, even in the case of a Moses and an Abraham, w see that each one of us can be enabled by the same fai to accomplish the work which God places before us, : they accomplished the work which God gave them.

These works are varied; but the principle by which Gc accomplishes them in each person is the same: it is simpl divine, and all-powerful. Let us not be astonished at thi It seems astonishing at first that the simple fact that Gc hears and answers our prayers may accomplish such ma vels, and indeed the will of God realised in the humble

Christian is no less a marvel than the crossing of the Red Sea, and all other miracles. But when we reflect for a moment, we understand the power which is of the very nature of faith. What a marvellous thing, that you and I, although placed in the midst of a world steeped in sin, although drawn by sight, sense, and self-will to follow the evidence of our organs—that we can deny all that and believe against hope, against experience, against sight, irresistible sight, believe one word, only a little word which God speaks to us! Remember what Luther said: "Ein Wörtlein kann inh fällen" (a little word can make one fall) and if faith means that this little word of God penetrates into our hearts, it is not surprising that faith is all-powerful, because it is not surprising that God should do all that He wills to do. But how can we obtain this faith, so great in its effects, and so wonderful in its nature that it can only be the result of a creative act of God in our souls—so that the man who believes is a more astonishing phenomenon than a new world formed by the hand of God. How can we obtain it? By asking: God gives to him who asks. But let us take care here, my dear friends. One could believe that such faith is easy to obtain, if all we have to do is to pray to God for it. No! the gifts of God are not offered as cheaply as that. Sometimes, undoubtedly, to show what He is, God is pleased to create all of a sudden a new man in answer to a single prayer: but that is not His normal method. This faith, although granted in answer to our prayers, is the result of a long and laborious conquest, and is worth it all. But God will have us strive to obtain it. Adam in his *Thoughts* says something very true: "Prayer is the easiest work of all: but the prayer of faith is the hardest of all."

We shall attain to such faith by being often on our knees; praying over and over again, showing God that we realise how costly it is and adding to our prayer such exercise of heart, that we first of all obtain a little faith, by which we shall be encouraged on to a more fervent prayer, which in turn will obtain for us a new faith—that is how we shall come to it. There are three things we must do to grow in faith: ask for it; exercise it; see it exemplified in the great saints as we study deeply the Scriptures. We cannot hope to obtain anything from God if we do not realise the price of it.

And here in a few words is the application I wish to make of what I have just said. You must gather faith for the future, you must labour today for the faith which you will need in five, ten, twenty years' time. You must store up day by day this spiritual provision, so that when the strength even to pray declines and when your languishing body and oppressed spirit help but little in the terrible conflict of which faith is the prize and reward, then surrounded by the superabounding gifts of God, all you will have to do is to open your eyes and stretch out your hand! Oh! do not wait until then to acquire faith: you may indeed still find it; but let us apply ourselves to prepare for such moments of supreme conflict by increasing our provision more and more and growing up every day in faith.

My friends, I am in a position where nothing matters to me except faith. As our brother was just saying in his prayer, by it we have power, peace and joy. It is, alas, easy to say and preach from a distance that faith must triumph over all. But when you must fight hand to hand with the enemy, when everything is at stake, even following Jesus, in the morning into the desert, in the evening to Gethsemane, and then the next afternoon to Golgotha—you then realise how serious it is. But blessed be God, eternally blessed! you would misunderstand me if you thought that, because I speak in this way, God does not uphold me. He upholds me wonderfully. But I would have you know in advance how stern the combat is, much sterner than I believed before passing through it myself—that you may do what I have done in my own small way, and wish it were much more; that you may grow day by day in faith, that you may live only to grow in faith; that you may be before God only men of faith and prayer, preparing yourselves by fulfilling His will today for the fulfilment of His will tomorrow. Oh! how my sufferings would be sweetened, how they *are* sweetened by the thought that they are useful to you, that the words which I address to you in my infirmity have reached your hearts by the Holy Spirit!

O my friends! if this little handful of men that we make up here were men of faith, there would be many eleventh chapters of Hebrews to write without leaving this upper room!

IX

JESUS CHRIST OUR EXAMPLE IN SUFFERING

[9 December 1855]

IN the presence of Jesus Christ who feeds us with His flesh and His blood, and who feeds us continually by faith, I feel in my heart led to address a few words to those who suffer. I am sure that, however small my audience may be, my words will fall on soil prepared to receive them. We all suffer. Those who suffer most are not always those who appear to suffer most. There is pain which is known to God and unknown to men, but in any case, anyone who feels, who thinks and believes, well knows what pain is.

There is something in pain which is contrary to our nature, and to which we find it very difficult to become accustomed for it seems to us that we ought always to be happy. This sentiment is an entirely legitimate one; it honours the goodness of our Creator. It is perfectly true that we ought to be quite exempt from pain and always full of joy; but sin has upset all that, and now that which is contrary to nature has become natural. It enters into our view of God, into our very make-up, and into our eternal interests, that we should suffer in diverse ways. You know how the Book of Job gathers together and classifies the principal sufferings of life: the loss of possessions, the loss of dear ones and the loss of health, which was kept till last. This order is, of course, of Satan, who is an expert in temptations! If at this moment the hearts of all here present were to be opened, what sufferings we should have to recount to God!

Well then, my dear friends, I would have absolutely nothing to say to you to console you, if I could not take the

Word of God. There is no consolation in nature: she explains nothing, she understands nothing, hopes nothing, expects nothing. And even her hope and her expectation are vain. But I am full of things to tell you as I contemplate the cross of Jesus Christ, around which we gather to celebrate the memory of His sacrifice. It means, as you well know, that we are purified from our sins by His blood, redeemed by His bitter sacrifice, our sins being atoned for by His cross, in the simplest, easiest-to-understand and yet most profound way, all at the same time, Jesus Christ being the propitiatory victim who reconciles us to God by His death. There is the foundation of the Gospel, there is the heart of it: and, apart from that, there is only a poor faded Gospel, lacking in power. But in the light of the cross, pain changes its aspect completely, in proportion to our faith. Jesus Christ, the Son of God, appeared in the world. How did He appear? As a joyful man? No, as a man of sorrows. Now here is a wonderful thing, something amazing and extraordinary, the Son of God appearing on the earth, is presented not just as one who suffers, but as the one who suffers what no man can conceive of suffering. The cross of Jesus Christ is the centre of all pain and suffering; it absorbs all and there is none which it does not explain, which does not flow from it, as it were, naturally.

My dear friends, when we remember that Jesus Christ has suffered for us, and consider that all we suffer is a mark of resemblance to our Saviour, and that, by the infinite character of His sufferings, the more we suffer, then the more we resemble Him, surely, does not that change the nature of pain? This thought that Jesus has borne it before us, that He could not be spared it, is it not illuminating and at the same time sweet? And who is he, however low he may be stricken, who will not be sustained by this thought: "My Saviour was like this: it is a sign that I am like Him. Now I know that I belong to Him, He is calling me and I am beginning to enter into the purposes of God and to understand something of His ways. My cross is united with

His cross and my sufferings with His sufferings." This is the application of what St. Paul said: "For whom he did foreknow, he also did predestinate to be conformed to the image of his Son, that he might be the firstborn among many brethren. Moreover, whom he did predestinate, them he also called; and whom he called them he also justified: and whom he justified, them he also glorified." He desired us to be "conformed to the image of his Son," and the context shows that it means essentially a conformity in suffering. That, then, is one first thought which is powerful to sustain us; it is that pain is an essential part of the life of Jesus Christ and is thus a mark of resemblance to Him. Here is another. Why did Jesus Christ suffer? To atone for sin. Now pain is presented to us as a just consequence of sin. We cannot bear the pains which Jesus has borne; but we shall be happy in the feeling that righteousness has been fully vindicated when we bear our part. "Why does mortal man afflict himself because of his sins?" The following passage from St. Peter: "Forasmuch then as Christ hath suffered for us in the flesh, arm yourselves likewise with the same mind: for he that hath suffered in the flesh hath ceased from sin," shows us that, in order to make us break with our sins, we must suffer. Sin and pain must of necessity be set in relation to each other in us personally and pain must be employed to destroy sin in us, not as a means of atonement—that is only found in Jesus Christ—but that we may learn to associate pain with sin. Likewise, joy with sanctification and deliverance. Indeed, this thought that pain is a fruit of sin serves to sustain us, because it makes us consider pain as a common and natural path, which we cannot and ought not to be spared.

And finally, why did Jesus Christ suffer as an atonement for sin? To save us and make us partakers of eternal glory, by love; that is the thought which is uppermost in the sufferings of the Saviour. Well, then, our pain should be a pain of love, and not of egoism, not drawing attention to ourselves, but contributing to the glory of God first and foremost, and then contributing to the spiritual well-being of our neighbour. Through the example he can give in his sufferings, through the patience given him by God to enable him to bear them, there are treasures of love and the power of love in pain borne by a Christian. What a sweet and heavenly thought that we can be useful to our fellows in our sufferings, and above all to our brethren! There is something too which can bring our sufferings even closer to those of Christ. It is the thought expressed by St. Paul when he says in a passage which I love to quote: "I fill up in my body that which cometh behind in the sufferings of Christ for his body's sake, that is the Church." I will not enter into the explanation of this verse which presents some difficulties: certainly nothing was further from the apostle's mind than the thought that he was suffering to atone for sin, but he unites his sufferings with those of the Saviour, and because He suffered to save us, Paul suffers for the good of humanity, as he wrote to Timothy, "In doing these things, thou wilt save not only thyself, but also those which hear thee".

This, then, is what sustains a Christian who experiences pain. Jesus Christ suffered; the more I suffer, the more I am like Him; pain is therefore a privilege. Jesus Christ suffered for sin; pain is a necessary and salutary fruit of sin. Then lastly, Jesus Christ suffered in order to save, and I must suffer to be a means of blessing to men, and lead souls captive to the obedience of the cross. Let all those who suffer apply themselves to getting out of themselves and renouncing a selfish attitude to pain, which is without faith, without love and without consolation; let them enter fully into the love of Christ, so that their suffering also may be like a cross planted in the earth, under whose shadow all those around may shelter, not to give them eternal life, but to show them the way which leads to it, for the glory of God. To Him be the glory in all ages! Let us rejoice in Him, and let us say that by the power of faith and love there is no pain which cannot be borne peaceably and happily and related to the glory of God and the welfare of men, and so much for our eternal consolation that in Heaven we shall consider it a great privilege to have suffered much under the cross of Jesus! Amen.

X

SIN

[16 December 1855]

DEAR friends, this Communion sets before our eyes memories of the deepest imaginable joy; but let us not forget that as Jesus Christ walked towards glory and towards the resurrection by way of the cross, this joy can be felt only by those who have first felt the bitterness of sin. It is in proportion to the liveliness of the feeling we have of the bitterness of sin. O my friends, what is sin? Who among us can comprehend how criminal it is, how bitter, what dreadful judgments it naturally entails, and how absolutely necessary it is for us to be washed and freed from it completely before we can enjoy a moment's rest. It seems to me that it belongs to those who experience especially deep suffering, and who are called upon to meditate constantly on the mystery of a God full of love who sends His children suffering upon suffering—it seems to me that it belongs to them to meditate more especially upon the depths of sin.

Take a man such as François Gonthier of Nyon. For my part I never knew a man who, as far as one can humanly judge, was more advanced in true and solid Christian piety; the sort which unites purity of faith with humility of spirit and charity. Well, this man who seemed to deserve to be filled with all the comforts of God, was filled with all His most bitter dispensations. He lost successively his only son, his tenderly-loved wife and his twelve-year-old daughter who alone reminded him of his lost treasures. Left alone as he was, it transpired that God purposed to make his solitude even more complete, by taking away first a beloved sister and then a young niece of twenty, on whom all his affections were concentrated; and I have not said all. In addition to that, his health deteriorated so profoundly that he said to me one day: "Do you know how I compose my books? Just as you get the goodness out of orange-peel—by pressing it, until at length you make the juice come out drop by drop". He experienced extreme weakness, and almost continual pain, which constantly increased so that his misery only grew greater until the end of his life. When I think of such an existence, I say to myself, What is sin?

I know well that one could reply that a man like Gonthier is stricken in order that his afflictions should instruct the Church by the patience and meekness of spirit with which he bore them, and this was assuredly his greatest consolation, because in this was his greatest resemblance to Jesus Christ. But God would not have sent all these sufferings to Gonthier only in the interests of others: one must not confuse the creature with the Creator; otherwise God would make man a saviour. In the case of Jesus Christ—He struck Him for the sin of mankind, but in our case, He never strikes us with a measure of suffering which our personal sins have not merited. Indeed, our sin merits over and above what we suffer, and even beyond what we conceive of suffering. That is what the Scripture teaches us, especially the Psalms, on every page. David cannot deal with the subject of his sufferings without almost imperceptibly slipping into a consideration of his sins. You can see this particularly as you read over again the thirty-eighth Psalm, where bit by bit he mixes his sufferings in with his sins, in such a way that one can hardly distinguish between them. What, then, is sin? What horror does it present before the eyes of God? What punishment does it make necessary? With what ransom can it be expiated?

Consider next sin in an ordinary Christian, who has never risen to such heights of Christian living as Gonthier did; who goes through life as best he may without dishonouring his profession, but who has not felt the bitterness of sin; who has afflictions because one always has them, but who has not learnt to convert his afflictions into a cross and unite his sufferings with those of his Saviour; and see all that there is in the heart of such a Christian, although he may be a sincere person, of latent sin, of hidden corruption, of secret infection which, if this heart were suddenly to open before us, would cause us to feel a frightful horror, on condition of course that we were able to feel the horror of sin, or in other words able to know all the holiness of the law of God, and all that His holiness requires by this formidable law. And then consider sin in the people of the world, who are steeped in sin, who since they came into the world have done nothing but drink it like water, breathe it like the air, who in their inner man are composed of sin, enveloped spiritually with a crust of sin which never a ray of life-giving, saving, sanctifying light has penetrated! What a gulf, what a tomb, what a spectacle before the eyes of God! Oh the thousands, yea millions of men spread throughout the whole world, in whom is found nothing but this frightful sin, of which they have only, at the most, a vague feeling which comes from time to time from God to plead with them to be converted, but they remain submerged in this dreadful and abominable state before God. Sin in the best Christians, sin in ordinary Christians, sin in the Church, sin in the world, O my friends, what misery! What is sin!

This is what Jesus Christ saw when he came down from Heaven to save us. We know nothing of it, but He knew; we felt nothing of it, but He felt it for us, and it is that which gave Him the strength to bear the anguish of the cross, the suffering of Gethsemane, the battles in the wilderness, and all the humiliations which had preceded it, of which His entire life was, as it were, made up. And now the sufferings which He has endured for us must become for us the measure of sin, as He Himself viewed it, and the depth of the abyss out of which He drew us. None of us has any idea, no, my friends, none of us has any idea what sin really is! None of us knows sin, because none of us fully knows the Saviour, nor His sufferings, nor His love.

O my friends, in the presence of this blood poured out and flesh broken, let us learn what sin is, what the peril of our souls, to make us flee for refuge near to Jesus and seek in Him alone what He alone can give us. Let us assure our hearts that only Holy Scripture can teach us. Our personal meditations will never reveal to us what sin is, and this is a point where I feel particularly the necessity and the reality of the divine inspiration and authority of the Scriptures, because we could never learn to know sin otherwise than by obedience to an external authority superior to us, independent of our feelings, on which we ought certainly to meditate with heart-searching and fervent prayers. But the illuminating truth comes from on high, given especially by the Spirit of God speaking with the authority of God Himself. For we must begin by receiving the horror of sin, before we are yet capable of feeling it.

Well then, my friends, let us cast ourselves into the arms of the Saviour. Will the sufferings and pains of this world hold us back? And have we in any case time to be preoccupied with them, when we have our souls to save? Let us go to Jesus with a feeling of profound humiliation, but with an unreserved confidence in the one who has accomplished all and suffered all for us. O infinite sweetness, to rest fully at the foot of the cross! I am beginning to understand how great is my misery; but I embrace the cross of my Saviour. I desire only His cross, His grace, and His righteousness, and not the slightest admixture of my own works. My works! they could only condemn me; but redeemed by Him, washed in His blood, which has made an atonement for my sins, I seize His cross, and I lean only upon the sacrifice of my Saviour.

And then, let us speak of the Saviour to those who do not know Him. With such an evil, quite contrary to all earthly evils in that it is the only evil which is truly evil, and the root of all others, and with such a remedy in our hands, contrary to all earthly remedies in that it is the only sure and infallible one, can we go through life, encountering society, our families, our neighbours, our friends, without speaking to them about sin and about Jesus Christ who is their Saviour and ours? Let us seize hold of the cross. Let us die embracing it, proclaiming it, and our death will be the beginning of life, and God will be glorified in our bodies, whether by life, or by death, and before all by the blood and redemption of the Lamb of God. That is what I ask of God for each one of you, as I do so for myself, through the love of Christ which I implore Him to increase in us. Amen.

XI

THE CROSS REVEALS TO US THE LOVE OF GOD

[23 December 1855]

Psalm 88

MY good friends, you give me a very touching mark of your affection and brotherly sympathy in coming to share with me this supper of the Lord, which nourishes and strengthens my spirit and body week after week. The Psalm we read at the beginning of this service has a characteristic which makes it unique among all the Psalms: it is the only Psalm entirely of suffering without a word or even a trace of consolation. It is all black, all sombre, and you have to look very closely at it to discover a glimmer of hope in a name given to God in one of the first verses: "The God of our deliverance". Why this astonishing mystery? I can see two reasons for it.

The first is that God wants to make us see that although in the order of His mercy we never cry to Him without being delivered, and between the moment we suffer the most frightful agony and the moment we find the most abundant consolation, there only needs to be the time it takes to read a few verses of a Psalm, as for example in Psalm thirteen, yet sometimes the Lord sees fit to let us cry for a certain time without an answer, without consolation, without even a glimmer of hope to relieve our distress. It is then that we must feed upon faith alone, and with Jeremiah, with David and with all the saints who have been tried in this way, we must wait on Him, ask Him why He is hiding His face, and in spite of the cloud which veils Him from us, never doubt Him. In one hundred and fifty Psalms there is one Psalm only which teaches us that lesson as if it cost the Lord's love dearly to give us this warning.

But there is a second reason for this Psalm, which is indeed very close to the first. You know how the Psalms are full of the Messiah. It is Christ who is speaking and depicting His suffering, and we find in Psalm eighty-eight the same Saviour who speaks that word in Psalm twenty-two: "Eloi, Eloi, lama sabachthani"—"My God, my God, why hast thou forsaken me?" followed soon by that other word: "Nevertheless thou art holy, who hearest the afflicted when he cries unto thee". Thus from this Psalm we see that the Saviour's distress was so excessive that it surpasses all that men, and even the most afflicted of His servants, can—I do not say feel—but even conceive. And why was this? Because God is love. The answer is strange, but true. God is love: but for us, my dear friends, however loaded we may be with the gifts of God, whether temporal or spiritual, or of whatever kind—though we have His Word, His promises, and everything else—something is still wanting, if we may so speak, to enable the love of God to find its way to our heart—and that is suffering. We know that God does not suffer; that He is incapable of it; that He is raised above suffering, as above temptation and all the sorrows of earth; and to make us understand the love of God in all its fulness and its reality, it was necessary that God should manifest Himself to our view so as to prove to us His love by His sufferings, since man could never have been persuaded, or rather never could have been won, otherwise.

Jesus Christ then, the Son of God, Himself God, became the Son of Man in order to be capable of suffering, and thus show us the love of God in a form capable of breaking the hardest hearts, even though they take little heed. Jesus came upon the earth to suffer. How well He accomplished this task! He began by taking a body similar to our sinful body; and who among us can conceive all the self-denial, the humiliation, the sacrifice, that the Lord of glory, the Prince of life, underwent, in lowering Himself to the misery of our poor nature, and taking upon Him all its degradation, even to that of the tomb? "Who being in the form of God, thought it not robbery to be equal with God; but made himself of no reputation, and took upon him the form of a servant. . . . He became obedient unto death, even the death of the cross." And notice that what distinguishes the sorrows and sufferings of Jesus Christ from ours is that He chose them and took them upon Himself voluntarily. Nothing obliged Him to do it; He chose them, and took them upon Himself one after another, to perform His Father's will, but to perform it freely. And why? For us; because He could not bear the thought of the eternal misery into which sin had brought us. My God, what love, what love!

I pass rapidly over all His career of suffering and humiliation and I come to His Gethsemane. You enter the garden of Olives in the middle of the night, and you see a man prostrate with His face on the ground; He is weeping and crying. Perhaps you would take Him for a fool—but it is your Saviour! Consider even in His posture, His prayer and His tender reproaches addressed to His disciples, the immensity of His suffering, suffering which we are no more capable of understanding or conceiving than God and the infinite, because there is not only the physical and external suffering; there is also a spiritual suffering which we could not possibly bring ourselves to understand. Not only the saints, but even men who do not know the Lord, have patiently suffered the most atrocious pains; but the infinite sufferings of Jesus meant for Him—inner secret pains into which we cannot penetrate—that of bearing alone before a holy God the weight of our sins, the innocent for us guilty, and of finding Himself (although I hardly dare touch on this mystery) as if separated for a moment from the love of the Father, if one can speak thus, although He was one with Him; and constrained to cry: "My God, my God, why hast thou forsaken me?"

Why did He suffer thus? Sinner, for you, for you; and He so loved you that even if there were only you on this earth to save, He would have entered into His Gethsemane for you. My God, what love, what love! See Him finally, on the cross. I will say no more on the subject; how could I describe such a mystery, even if I had the strength? I take my place with you at the foot of the cross, and I contemplate the sufferings of my Saviour. And I ask you to observe this; that, at the moment when He was given up to that frightful anguish, to that agony which no man could know, or conceive, or even dimly perceive, He towers above the suffering in order to glorify God and to save men to the uttermost; and it is from the depth of that agony that we hear words such as these, "Father, forgive them for they know not what they do", and again, "Woman, behold thy son", "Disciple, behold thy mother". My God, what love, what love!

Last Sunday, at the foot of the cross, we were contemplating what a view it gives us of the horror, the enormity and the terrors of sin! Today how sweet to contemplate the sufferings of our Saviour and the view they give us of the greatness and the incomprehensible depth of the love of God. Oh! my friends, if we always have this love before our eyes, all will be explained to us, even the most cruel sufferings, since they are only the sequel in His own to what He has suffered. At the same time everything will become sweet and easy for us. Faith makes all things possible, love makes all things easy! "His commandments are not grievous." With our minds full of this picture of the love of the Saviour, and the love of God revealed in the Saviour, as we read thereby in the heart of the Father the love of God for us, we will abandon ourselves to the Lord to do and to suffer all that He deems good to send us. Ask God for the grace to fill our minds with this thought: "God is love", and in order to do this let us keep at the foot of the cross of our Saviour and never lose sight of it, till after we have suffered a little, seeing that is necessary, He will take us by the hand and with Him we shall cross the interval from the Friday to the Sunday morning, be raised with Him and be set up with Him in the glory-land where He awaits us and where we shall bless Him all the more that we have suffered with Him, and above all that we have suffered for His Name! Amen.

XII

THE UNSEEN THINGS

[30 December 1855]

Revelation 22

THE chapter which has just been read to us would be sufficient by itself to fill our hearts at all times with strength and joy, if we could receive it with absolute simplicity of faith. If a man hard-pressed by poverty was assured that tomorrow he would make his fortune; if a man borne down by sufferings was assured that tomorrow he would enter into a life of well-being; would they not be sustained by this hope to be patient for a short time, and would it not make the hours which separated them from the time of their happiness pass rapidly by?

And if we, my friends, had a simple and firm faith and a clear view of this eternal felicity which is described for us in terms so beautiful and so touching in the last chapter of Revelation, would we not also say, "Lord Jesus, come!" and would we not say it with complete peace of mind? What do we need more than God has given to us? Nothing which God cannot give us: a simple faith in things unseen. We live in time, it is only a question of living in eternity. We are constantly drawn towards the things which are seen, it is only a question of entering into communion with the unseen. I say, it is only a question of that; but that is a big thing, it involves an immense change. For that which constitutes sin is not only the crude form of disobedience to the divine law which rules the world; what constitutes sin at its source in a subtle and profound manner is unbelief, the allurement of material things. For because God is invisible, and the centre and soul of the invisible world, it is only too easy for us to feed ourselves on the visible material things because we are naturally alienated from God. It is of the very nature of the Word of God that it lives and moves in the midst of the invisible world; and that alone, for a thinking man, should be sufficient proof of its inspiration. It is not given to man, enslaved through his fallen nature by material things, to raise himself above them as the Word of God does. To do this he would need to go outside of himself in order to lift himself up to the unseen world. But the Word of God does this very thing as indeed Jesus Christ the Son of Man does, who being in Heaven speaks of Heaven, and not only He but also those men who were the instruments charged with the transmission of the Word of God, which being filled with Jesus Christ speaks of Heaven although it is upon earth, by that miracle of the grace of God which we call inspiration and which constitutes the authority of that Word. The result is a pure book, a holy book, a book of God, a book which is raised above us and above the world, which speaks to us of another world, and speaks to us from the very heart of that other world! How can we be put in touch with things unseen? At this point we all feel our need and our infirmity: but do we realise what would be our power, our felicity, our peace and our joy if we could only live and move in the midst of the unseen world, like the Word of God and Jesus Christ; if we could be conveyed by the power of faith to God Himself and the things of God, and see things as God sees them, measure them as He measures them, appreciate them as He appreciates them, and judge them as He judges? "If we would judge ourselves, we should not be judged", as someone has just read from His Word.

From what we have just seen we may conclude that the first means of entering into communion with the unseen world is to live with the Holy Scriptures, which are the Word and testimony of God. By living with them I do not mean only reading them every day and receiving their witness; I mean feeding on them, seeking in them the bread of life which has come down from Heaven, and seeking the

Lord Jesus Christ Himself, that life-giving bread who gives life to the world and whose body was broken for you, for me, for us all; and receiving it by faith, particularly through the sacrament of the Lord's Supper, which places the object of faith so vividly before our eyes. We must feed upon the Word of God, my dear friends, live constantly with it, day and night.

May it be to us what it was, to quote but one example, for the author of Psalm one-hundred and nineteen. This Psalm has a hundred and seventy-six verses and there are only one or two in which the Word of God is not mentioned—under one or other of the innumerable names which the Psalmist gives to it. Oh! let us live with the Word of God! May we be constantly surrounded by the atmosphere of the Scriptures, for it is the atmosphere of Heaven and of God Himself!

Again, to enter into communion with things unseen, let us pray without ceasing. Yes, pray: but how? O my God! How can we pray as seeing Thee, speaking to Thee, listening to Thee, replying to Thee, conscious of Thy presence, and taking pleasure in Thy Word? Oh! who beside Thee will teach us to pray, Thou God of prayer? My God, forgive the manner in which Thy Church prays, which alone in the world knows what it is to pray; forgive the way in which we ourselves pray; this languor, uncertainty, unbelief, even at those times in our Christian life and ministry when we are least unfaithful and least unbelieving! My God, pardon the sin of our holy offerings! Ah! if only we could at this very moment span, by means of prayer, the distance which separates us from Thee; if we could only pray as Jesus Christ prayed, as Moses prayed, or Samuel, or David, or St. Paul, or St. John! If only we could pray in a way that really could be called praying, as St. James expresses it, speaking of Elijah; "He prayed in praying"! Alas! most of the time we pray without praying. We do not realise the feebleness and unbelief that is in our prayers, because we do not live with invisible things; nor do we realise the great blessings and graces of which we deprive ourselves. O my friends, let us say this prayer over and over again, "Lord, teach us to pray!" When we know how to pray, then we shall know all things, and better still, we shall have all things. We shall know Jesus Christ and we shall do better than that, we shall possess Him. Besides, you can only know Him as you possess Him. It is in possessing Him that you come to know Him, and in coming to know Him that you come to love Him. And with Him you triumph by faith over the things that are seen, and crush Satan under your feet. May the God of peace Himself crush Satan under our feet!

My friends, the things which are unseen, the things of the last chapter of the Revelation! . . . Soon we shall all appear before God. This is true not only of those who expect to be called, from one day to another, who are more especially warned by the Lord to hold themselves in readiness, and who rejoice—Oh! yes, those who ardently long for the moment when Jesus will say to them: "Come!"—but this is true of everyone, since none of us can be sure that he will live until tonight. It is now, while you have the use of all your faculties, that you must enter into communion with the things that are unseen, by the Word of God and by prayer. These things of which I speak to you are really quite old: but alas! they are also quite new to us because of our apathy and unbelief! . . . Seek the things which are unseen. Seek God Himself in the midst of that unseen world, by Jesus Christ who has drawn aside the veil, that is to say by His broken body, and whose love and suffering are the measure of that joy which He has prepared for us! If He tarry, "wait for Him, for He will come and will not tarry".

XIII

THE MAN OF SORROWS AND MEN OF SORROW

[6 January 1856]

THE Christian who experiences affliction is directly called of God to meditate on the place of affliction in the plan of divine redemption, in the extension of the kingdom of God on earth, and in the revelation given to us in the Holy Scriptures. Then he will begin to understand this simple and at the same time profound word: "Think it not strange . . . as though some strange thing happened to you. . . ." It would indeed be strange if we could be matured for eternal life or, more particularly, if a servant of God could experience blessing in his work, I do not just say without afflictions, but without a great deal of affliction: for, "It is by much tribulation that we must enter the kingdom of God".

This doctrine is first clearly revealed to us in the very one whose sacrifice we are now celebrating, since eternal life could not be ours save through His sufferings and His sacrifice. The Saviour was "a man of sorrows, and acquainted with grief"; not only a man of sorrows, but *the Man* of Sorrows, in whom all sufferings are united and who has suffered what no other man can suffer or even imagine. But as the Master, so the disciples; and the disciples of our Saviour Jesus Christ—I speak more especially of those inspired instruments in whom the Lord has been in a more particular way manifested and reproduced—they have all made up a series of "men of sorrows", from Abel down to St. Paul and St. John. This does not strike us sufficiently from a superficial study of Scripture. But when you study the Word of God a little more deeply, you are more and more struck by it. The apostles and the prophets are presented to us throughout Scripture as men of sorrows, and of sorrows greater than we know or see, for the Scripture only lets us glimpse, rather than shows us fully. For in order to show us what these men of God suffered, every detail of their lives would have had to be recounted.

Of the apostles there is only one whose life is given to us in any detail. But here is a man whose ministry God has defined in terms of suffering, since He said in calling him: "I will show him how great things he must suffer for my name's sake" (Acts 9.16). If we follow the course of St. Paul's life, we find that it is from beginning to end a life of sufferings, without and within. Listen to what he himself says: (2 Cor. 11.23-33.)

> Are they ministers of Christ? (I speak as a fool) I am more; in labours more abundant, in stripes above measure, in prisons more frequent, in deaths oft.
>
> Of the Jews five times received I forty stripes save one.
>
> Thrice was I beaten with rods, once was I stoned, thrice I suffered shipwreck, a night and a day I have been in the deep;
>
> In journeyings often, in perils of waters, in perils of robbers, in perils by mine own countrymen, in perils by the heathen, in perils in the city, in perils in the wilderness, in perils in the sea, in perils among false brethren;
>
> In weariness and painfulness, in watchings often, in hunger and thirst, in fastings often, in cold and nakedness.
>
> Beside those things that are without, that which cometh upon me daily, the care of all the churches.
>
> Who is weak, and I am not weak? who is offended, and I burn not?
>
> If I must needs glory, I will glory of the things which concern mine infirmities.
>
> The God and Father of our Lord Jesus Christ, which is blessed for evermore, knoweth that I lie not.
>
> In Damascus the governor under Aretas the king kept the city of the Damascenes with a garrison, desirous to apprehend me:
>
> And through a window in a basket was I let down by the wall, and escaped his hands.

Ponder every detail by itself. What a picture! What a life, without and within! See the measure of his love in the extent of his sufferings.

Now the prophets: "Take the prophets, who have spoken in the name of the Lord, for an example of patience", says St. James. And if we study the life of the prophets at all seriously, especially those whose history we know least imperfectly, we will find his statement exactly true. This is so for Jeremiah, to take one example of whom we do know something. But the best known of all the prophets, whose life-story is given in the fullest detail, is David. Have you ever thought about the sufferings with which the life of David was filled? If you take his life as it is related to us in the Books of Samuel, Kings and Chronicles, you will not know anything about them. There you see David as a man who in his early days was pursued by Saul. He had many enemies, but after all he triumphed over Saul and entered into great glory. Then you see him deeply troubled and afflicted in his own family life, as a just consequence of his sins. But you also see him abundantly comforted and upheld by God, who, even in His most awful punishments, still remembers His promises to David and His mercy towards him. It is a life in which we find many trials and anxieties; but in the end we are not given much idea of the sufferings of David. To know these, we must read the Psalms. The Psalms reveal the inner man of David, and in his inner life they reveal, so to speak, the inner life of all the prophets of God: indeed, the Psalms are full of expressions of the most unheard of suffering. There David speaks continually of his ills, his sicknesses and his numberless enemies. It is difficult to understand what he means by these enemies, to whom he refers continually; but they do at least speak to us of an inner conflict, the reality of which we could never doubt, even if we had within our hands as evidence only the story of David. Read Psalm thirty-eight: read and ponder every thought.

Innumerable enemies who press upon him, the feeling of his sins which overwhelms him, this complexity of sicknesses: he is afflicted by his eyes, which are blinded; inflammation of the kidneys; his back bent, so that he can hardly walk; sores which run and give out a foul odour—that is David in this Psalm. But if you read Psalm six, if you read Psalm sixty-nine and many other Psalms, you will find him in similar affliction. Truly, he is a man overwhelmed with sorrows. We must not say that because David was a type of Jesus Christ these sufferings only applied to the Messiah.

They were without doubt a type of the sufferings of Jesus Christ; but they could only be a type of the sufferings of Messiah because they were actual sufferings; and precisely because David was a man of sorrows, he was a type of the Man of Sorrows.

But my dear friends, shall we stay there? After recognising that the apostles and the prophets were men of sorrows, shall we end there on that sad note of suffering? They were not only men of sorrows, but they were men who overcame suffering and made their sufferings further the glory of God. At their head, Jesus Christ triumphs over suffering and pursues His mission of love even to the most cruel agonies. In Gethsemane, we hear Him exhorting His disciples, and when it came to fulfilling His message of love in their very presence, He preserved all His liberty of spirit. It was the same on the cross where He did not lose one opportunity of giving His disciples, the people, John, Mary and everyone lessons concerning eternal life until the end of His frightful agony. The Man of Sorrows was triumphing over suffering, to accomplish in His sufferings and by His sufferings His great mission. It is the same with His disciples, and also with the apostles. What use does St. Paul make of his sufferings? He relates them all to the glory of God. He is not at all overwhelmed by them, as we are so easily. He triumphs over them by the love of Christ, and makes them all serve for the advancement of the kingdom of God with a wonderful faithfulness.

And David, on whom I have dwelt more especially—have you noticed how he triumphs over suffering in order to accomplish his work? The main object of the mission which David received from God for all generations in the Church was the composition of the Psalms. Indeed, he composed his Psalms, or a great part of them, in the midst of the most cruel sufferings. Just imagine that, overwhelmed by suffering, physical, moral and spiritual, you were called to write a psalm, and that in the very midst of all these sufferings and at the very time when they were like those described in Psalm thirty-eight, hymns began to ring out to the glory of God and for the instruction of the Church! How David triumphs over himself, and how humiliating it is for us who, in our weakness, are obliged in most instances to wait until our sufferings are past before we can gather the fruit of them, both for ourselves and others! But David in his sufferings writes his Psalms. He writes Psalm thirty-eight while he suffers persecutions, inner torments, the bitterness of sin. I know that one could say that David wrote Psalm thirty-eight in cold blood, by taking himself back in mind to sufferings which he no longer experienced; as a poet can transport himself into sufferings which he has never experienced at all. But no, this idea is as repugnant to you as it is to me: it was in the furnace, in the very heart of the furnace, that he wrote these lines which were to serve for the encouragement of the Church in all time. O power of the love of Christ! O renunciation of self-will! O grace of the true servant of God! O virtue of the apostle and of the prophet, virtue of Christ in them and of the Holy Spirit! For man would never be capable of such strength of will and of such a triumph over the flesh.

My dear friends, I leave each one of you to apply this for himself. It can be done by asking two questions: Are we men of sorrows, and to what extent do we share in the afflictions of Christ? When we share in the afflictions of Christ can we triumph over them and relate them by the power of love to the glory of God, and the benefit of our neighbour and our brethren; and do they at the same time work even more for our sanctification and spiritual sustenance, and to gather for us the treasure of an excellent glory?

XIV

A DYING MAN'S REGRETS

I. THE SECRET OF AN ACTIVE AND PEACEFUL HOLY LIFE

[13 January 1856]

MY beloved in the Beloved of the Father, I thank God who has permitted me once again to speak to you in His Name for your encouragement and for my own consolation. But I must ask you to exercise toward me the patience of God, who is pleased to accept a man, "according to what he hath, not according to what he hath not". My declining strength will not allow me either to sit up or to turn round, and therefore I can only stay in this position to speak to you. I hope I shall be distinct enough for you all to hear.

A man is in a singular position indeed who, for quite a few months already and perhaps for quite a time yet—how long he knows not—is living constantly with the thought that his links with this life have been broken, that he is incurably and mortally stricken of God, and that he does not know at what moment the Father's voice will call him home. He would indeed be heartless, unthinking and devoid of all Christian feeling not to glance over his past life; and at the same time he is brought to ask himself, with thoughts of the possibility of recovery mounting in his soul—as they are bound to; for, after all, he is in the hands of God who raises the dead—this question: "If my life was given back to me, what use would I make of it?" And reminding himself of the weakness and frailty of his resolutions, which a life-time has demonstrated to him, he would nevertheless hope that in the goodness of God such a visitation would not be lost on the second part of his life and ministry.

Then I say to myself (for I am that man): I would do such and such a thing; and assuredly there is not one thing that I would not wish to do otherwise or better than I have done. It is a salutary humiliation for me and it can be a salutary instruction for you, to consider the regrets of a man who is dying or believes himself to be dying, and who figures to himself the different use he would make of his life, if it were restored to him.

It is more especially on such thoughts as these that I propose to dwell in these next addresses, and in order to choose an example straight away, here is a point on which, had I to begin afresh, I would make considerable changes in my life—I mean my inner life. It goes without saying that the more personal applications of the principle I have just laid down belong to the Lord; but there are more general applications which may without disadvantage be mentioned in a small meeting like this. For instance, prayer, Bible reading, Christian liberty. Now here is a point which strikes me: I regret having regulated my life too much by my own plans. I mean, by my plans of faithfulness and Christian sanctification and not more simply by the plan which the Lord unfolds before each of us. I think it will be easy for me to make you understand my idea in a few words, and every child of God will enter into it immediately. We are inclined to form for ourselves a certain ideal for the Christian life, Christian activity and the Christian ministry, and to attach to this ideal certain plans and certain methods, so much so that we are not satisfied unless we come to realise them; and thus it becomes important to make the best plans possible and to seek the best method of carrying them out. All of this is good, no doubt; but behind it all there is a fault: *self*—the hidden self, which has its roots in the depths of the heart, and which shows itself all too clearly in our best and purest works; while what I should wish to do is to take the plan of my life and daily conduct not from my own ideas and inclinations, but from the commandments of God, in His inward testimony, in the leading of His Spirit, and in the guidance He gives in the outward circumstances of our life.

My idea of how I would regulate my life will be understood perfectly, if you consider the way in which Jesus regulated His. In Jesus we do not find those plans and methods with which many good people have been taken up, and which have often tormented them so much, and taken up so much time, which could have been better employed. But what do we find? We find a man (I am considering Him here as Son of Man) who has no other desire than to accomplish the mission He received from the Father, and who has no other plan than to enter into the Father's plan; so that, with His eyes fixed on the Father, His only concern is to hear His voice in order to follow Him and to discover His will in order to carry it out. The good works which Jesus performs are all given to Him one after another, each one placed before Him by the hand of God upon His way. They follow each other so naturally and arise so easily, the one from the other, that there is no confusion, even on the busiest days of His ministry. During one day, for example, like the one which is described to us in the ninth chapter of St. Matthew, when He calls one of His apostles, heals some sick people, raises a dead man, and, as He passes by, heals a woman who has been ill for several years, without counting all the other benefits which He poured out everywhere on His journey, there is not a single moment of embarrassment or hesitation, either as to the way in which He performs His works, or as to the timing of each one of them, because Jesus Christ follows quite simply the plan of God and because God undertakes to guide Him.

When there is, on our side, this perfect accord with the will of God, He for His part gives us a perfectly clear light to guide us. In this way a wonderfully profound word from the Holy Spirit is realised: "We are created in Jesus Christ unto good works, which God has prepared before for us to walk in them." Here good works are presented to us not as a way that we have to make for ourselves, but as a way which God has made, and in which we have only to walk. It is God's way, not ours. We have only to follow this path, and we shall moment by moment perform the will of God.

If I have made you understand as well as I could, without going into detail, what I would have wished to do, and what I wish to do if my life should be restored to me, you will easily grasp the conclusion, what great advantages this conformity with the plan of God offers over keeping just to our personal plans, even the best of them. I add in passing that I have no thought of discouraging personal plans. We must seek to make them as good as possible, and I believe that our human frailty needs them as a support, provided that our personal plans are always subordinate to the general rule that we follow only the will of God.

Now, to limit myself to two or three main ideas, this way of which Jesus is the pattern, is first of all a condition of holiness. What is sin in essence? It is the seeking of self — self-confidence, self-will, self-righteousness, self-glory — and all that pertains to self. So the desire to do what is right and even to do the will of the Lord, founded upon plans and projects of our own making, partakes inevitably in some way or other of the root of sin; while, on the other hand, the very essence of holiness being the union of our will with the will of God, we shall only be in a state of true holiness when we have no other plan than God's plan and no other will than His will. Then only shall we be truly holy, with a holiness which has not only an outward appearance, but which has also an inward character, a holiness like that of Jesus Christ. His holiness follows and depends upon the principle I was expounding a moment ago, that is, constant abandonment to the will of God alone, manifested inwardly by the testimony of the Spirit, outwardly by the declarations of His Word and the signs of His Providence. Jesus Christ is holy, because He only desires what God wills; because He seeks not His own glory, but that of the Father. Therein lies the power of His holiness.

This conformity to the plan of God is, then, a condition of holiness; but it is at the same time a condition of activity. A tremendous amount of time may be lost in seeking our own self-interest even in what is good. It is well to consider how easily we may be mistaken and how we may be taken up with endless reflections and deliberations; and how many men have recognised at the end of their career that a considerable part of their life has been employed in forming plans, whereas they might have devoted it much more usefully to the work immediately at hand and for the good of others!

See what activity the plan of Jesus, which I quoted a moment ago, involves Him in. In the ninth chapter of St. Matthew and elsewhere we see good works in abundance thrown in His way, not one on top of another, but one after the other, and there is no limit to activity which is founded upon this perfect harmony with the will of God. Man's action then becomes divine action, and life becomes, as it were, divine life, throbbing in the heart of man, in which something is accomplished by the power of God. We have no idea of what we might do if we were completely swallowed up in this perfect harmony with God; if we sought no other will than His; if every word of our mouth, every beat of our heart, every thought of our intellect, every movement of our body and of our spirit were drawn towards Him, to wait on Him with the spirit of Samuel: "Speak, Lord, for thy servant heareth". There are some men—like Luther, Calvin, St. Paul, Moses—who have shown what a man can do when he seeks only the will of God. Jesus Christ has done much more, because in Him alone was conformity to the will of God perfect. It is, then, a condition of activity—of almost unlimited activity. Yet there are limits, since God does not demand of His creatures more than they are capable of doing.

Finally, and with this I conclude, it is a condition of peace. There is no peace for a man who finds the mainspring of his actions in his own will. He is always in danger of being mistaken; he is often troubled and in error, because human will and human interests are subject to much error; he has no rest, he is disturbed, he is tormented and inspires a deep compassion in anyone who sees his real desire to glorify God and yet also sees how he accumulates for himself obstacles in his way, by his lack of simplicity; while, on the other hand, when we look to God alone, we can cast all our burden upon Him and He sustains us. What is more, if my projects are of my own devising, they may be impossible to carry out. I might wish to follow a certain profession, but it involves expenses which are beyond my means. I might want to be a painter, but my sight is not good; or an orator, but I have no voice; or a surgeon, but my hand is not steady. I have missed my vocation, then, and there can be no consolation for me!

But there is no possibility of missing my vocation, if my projects are devised for me in the plan of God. For then, even this impossibility which I find of doing what I originally proposed to do, proves to me that God is not calling me to that; and the very infirmities which disqualify me become so many lights by which God reveals to me my true vocation. If we act in this spirit (I say it with deep reverence), our vocation is God's affair, not ours; and the activity, the individual exertion that God always requires of us, consists only in following Him in faithful and complete obedience. Thus we shall find perfect peace: God cannot mislead us.

Often we are disturbed by the thought that we are not doing enough, or that we are doing badly, or that we are not doing the work which God has given us to do. I recollect in particular how during the first weeks after I received the fateful verdict of the doctors, I was troubled by the thought that my work was not yet done. By the grace of God I am now delivered from that thought because I understand that it is not a question of my work, but of God's work: and I have come to recognise that even by the sufferings and afflictions which He has sent me and by the hope of eternal life which must follow them, the Lord has made me exercise another ministry, probably more important than that which I had in view and in any case more sure, because it comes to me directly from the hand of God, who mercifully constrains me to walk in this way for His service and for His glory. It is then that we shall be able to say, like Jesus Christ as He was about to die: "I have finished the work which thou gavest me to do". Why could He say that? Because He sought only to do the work of God, and God took Him, as you would pluck a ripe fruit, when His mission was accomplished.

Well then, let us also seek only to do the work which the Father has given us to do, and commit ourselves into His hands. We also, if we are faithful, shall only be taken when our work is done. God alone has the right to decide when the work He wants to do through us is finished. It may be very imperfect and incomplete in the eyes of man; but if we are upright before Him, He will not allow our life finally to end without leaving some traces upon earth. He will not take us until our work is accomplished before Him, and we shall then be able to say, like the Lord, in a spirit of humility: "I have finished the work which thou gavest me to do." Vinet said it without realising, when he gave his last lecture in theology on these words: "I have finished the work which thou gavest me to do." And what happened to Vinet, happened at the same time to Rochat, as it happens to all servants of God. There is a great peace in seeking one's plan only in God and in following Him—renouncing self. Only thus is peace to be found.

Let us, then, endeavour to seek our plans in God alone, so that those that are being called home may humble themselves and those who are still to remain alive may grow in grace. Let us, in this spirit, endeavour to follow Jesus Christ in His Gethsemane and to keep our eyes constantly fixed on the Father's will. It will be for us, as it was for Jesus Christ, a condition of holiness, of activity, and of deep peace. I pray God that you may have this peace. And I should be happy indeed, if I could think that these few meditations might have stimulated those who still have their life and strength before them, to use them so faithfully and so simply for the glory of God, according to their Saviour's example, that they might be able to say in their turn: "I have finished the work which thou gavest me to do," and that they might spend the rest of their life on earth in deep peace, waiting for the time when they will be called from this world to the Father, by the grace of the Lord, and by the virtue and unction of the Holy Spirit.

XV

A DYING MAN'S REGRETS

2. THE STUDY OF THE WORD OF GOD

[20 January 1856]

MY dear friends, the next regret of a dying man, in the same order of ideas which I started to expound last Sunday, concerns the new view which comes to him of the study of God's Word. Of the many things he wishes he had done, and would do otherwise, if he were recalled from his half-open grave, this is one of the most important. Ah! he certainly says then: How differently I ought to have acted with regard to the Word of God! How much more I ought to have studied it! How much better I ought to be acquainted with it, in order the more to live it out and communicate it to others! Let us pause a few moments upon this salutary thought which will serve to humble those for whom the end of time approaches, and to enlighten those to whom time is yet given, though how long they do not know.

What is Holy Scripture? Men will never be able to explain how it was formed, nor precisely how the Spirit of God and the spirit of man are combined in it, to make at the same time a divine Word, high as the heavens, and also a human word, quite near to us. That is no less difficult to explain than how the divine nature and the human nature are united in Jesus Christ: and this parallel is not mine, for Scripture calls itself the written Word, and Jesus Christ "the Word made flesh." Whatever may be the manner of their composition, the Holy Scriptures are Heaven speaking on earth. They are the maxims of the kingdom of Heaven communicated to men in human language, as if the invisible had descended into the midst of them, and were made visible to them. There is no other book, even of the best, which communicates to us the mysteries of the kingdom of Heaven, like the Bible. They are all more or less affected by human error; this alone is exempt from it: it is the book of God, full of the truth of God. In it we hear God speaking to us by the Holy Spirit. We see God, man, the present, the future, time and eternity described just as they are.

Whoever thus comes to understand what Scripture is will not find it difficult to admit what use he should make of it. We ought to interrogate the Scriptures as we would an angel from Heaven, sent by God at this very moment expressly to instruct us; or, still better, as we would interrogate our Lord Jesus Christ, if we had Him at this moment physically near us, and could speak to Him and hear Him speak. In fact we do speak to Him, and hear Him speak, when we read Holy Scripture, for it reveals Him, and on His behalf it reveals all things by His Spirit. Oh! how can we sufficiently venerate this book and give it the attention it deserves! True, the book itself is not the truth which saves us, it is the instrument of it. Likewise it is not salvation itself, but it reveals to us our salvation, and without it we could never have come to the knowledge of it. By the Scriptures also, the more we get to know them, the better we shall know Jesus as the Saviour of our souls. No Christian will contest the truth of this principle, and yet how few there are who really study the Scriptures! The greater number read them superficially, and limit themselves to some of the great leading truths, instead of penetrating more and more deeply, and, as far as possible, coming to know the whole, as it is written: "The secret things belong to the Lord; but those things which are revealed belong unto us and to our children for ever." (Deut. 29.29).

And why this strange contradiction? It is because of the difficulties which studying the Bible presents. We must agree that on beginning it, there are many difficulties and obscurities; and, as much labour is required to clear them up, and the mind of man is naturally idle and lazy, we lose courage little by little and limit ourselves to reading the same scriptures over and over again. This unvaried sort of study hardly penetrates beneath the surface, nor does it learn new things; but always going over the same things repeatedly, inspires in us a kind of weariness, as if the Word of God was not interesting—as if we could not always find some new instruction in it—as if it was not as inexhaustible as God Himself! Beware of thinking, however, that these difficulties are insuperable. No, my friends; but we must be prepared to take trouble; and there, as in prayer and in all parts of the Christian life, God wants man to be co-worker with Him. Knowledge of the Bible, taste for the Bible is the fruit and reward of this humble, sincere and persevering labour.

Ah! may each one go back to his Bible with a new vigour! Take book after book, seeking to gather from your study not only a general idea of outward piety, but a deep and growing knowledge of the kingdom of Heaven. Study a book until you have understood it as well as you are able; then take a second, and a third, and so on, and you will find that, on a second or a third reading, many of the difficulties which seemed insurmountable will disappear, and even though some may remain, you will not benefit the less from this labour which you have undertaken before God. In this study, do not leave any books out, even the most difficult; for example, the Minor Prophets, which many Christians leave on one side as unintelligible. If you take the trouble to study them, you will find a multitude of extremely interesting things in them. Besides, there are, through the goodness of God, good commentaries on certain parts of the Scriptures, which may serve as keys to the others; and by the help of these good books, we can enter more and more deeply into the knowledge of the Word of God. We will, of course, give special attention to those parts of the book that apply particularly to Christians, but,

I repeat, without neglecting any other part. This will be the fruit, the reward for those who will be thus faithful and persevering, to understand and to love the Word of God, to enter more and more deeply into it, and to find that time is always too short to complete our study of it. I knew a man who used to spend seven hours a day studying the Bible, and who found in this study an ever-growing delight.

If anyone, using by faith the resources which God puts at his disposal, and relying on God to guide him, follows out these thoughts of mine, which I can at this moment do little more than sketch, he will discover in the Word of God treasures which he never even suspected were there. Then it will become for him as firm a support as it was for Jesus, when He was tempted in the wilderness. And it will become for him what it was for the saints, in both the New Testament and in the Old Testament; what it was for David, and for Daniel, for Paul and all the saints of God.

May God give us all this blessing! and may He for whom it is no more difficult to bless in a little time than in a long time, or with little strength than with much strength, so make the words that I address to you penetrate into your hearts, that they will cause a transformation in your Bible study for which you will bless God for all eternity! Amen.

XVI

A DYING MAN'S REGRETS

3. THE USE OF TIME

[27 January 1856]

MY strength is exhausted, my dear friends, and I was wondering if today I should not remain silent. I will, however, say what I was going to say, limiting myself just to indicating the thoughts.

One of the things which trouble the Christian who thinks his end is near, or would trouble him if he were not at the foot of the cross, is the manner in which he has employed his time; and consequently this is one of the exhortations he must address to his brethren with their lives before them. It is written: "Redeem the opportunity"; this is a more exact rendering than the received one: "Redeem the time." "Redeem" here does not mean to buy over again, but to buy with alacrity the opportunity that God furnishes, for the days are evil; which means that the opportunity once lost may never come again. The good use of one's time is an idea so vast that it frightens the soul. There is something more modest about this thought: seize eagerly the opportunities that God provides, as they come from His hand. What a lot of opportunities are lost through idleness, unbelief, negligence, through selfishness, self-will, indecision, attachment to sin, and through a thousand other causes! I need not dwell upon that; there is no Christian whose heart does not condemn him, or whose conscience does not trouble him on this point. Ah! how sufficient and precious is the time God gives us! God, who is just, proportions the time to the work and the work to the time, and never gives us a good work to do for which time is lacking, nor does He give us a moment in which we have not some good thing to do. But how can we arrive at so filling up all our time that we do at least a part of the immense good that a single man could accomplish, if he put into practice this precept: "Whatsoever thy hand findeth to do, do it with thy might" (Eccles. 9:10), being constantly occupied in the service of the Lord? I want to give you two or three things to consider on that point, which I will leave to your conscience to develop.

First, we must be pervaded by the thought that we do not belong to ourselves, and therefore our time is not ours, any more than the rest of what we have. Our time belongs to God, and consequently we must look to God to ascertain what we have to do to fill the time which He gives us, and we must respond to the opportunities He presents to us. I assure you that sickness gives precious lessons on that, I mean concerning the fact that we belong not to ourselves, but to God. Our heart is naturally biased, and the root of sin is to make self the centre and aim of our life. But when you are ill and you suffer, how can you find consolation if the object of your life is in yourself? Your purpose in life has in that case completely failed. Sickness teaches us that we must look elsewhere for the purpose of life, than in ourselves; and that we live not just to be happy upon earth, but to glorify God. And this we can do in sickness as well as in health, often better. Let us, then, learn from all the sicknesses and sufferings of life, and from all that the Word of God teaches us, that our time belongs to God, and our only concern must be to use it for His glory.

Second, let us always be diligent in seizing the opportunities which God holds out to us. They will not fail us, and we shall find before us a life woven of good works, prepared and ready for us to walk in them; which are linked together and lead on the one from the other so easily, that our lives will be made up entirely of good works and obedience, and consequently, as we were just saying, joy and peace through the Holy Spirit. For this, we must have our eyes constantly opened and turned towards God, saying to Him, "Lord, here I am, what wilt Thou have me to do?" And when we have done one thing, "Lord, what wilt Thou have me to do now?" and so on without a single interval elapsing unfilled with the obedience we owe to God. God will furnish us accordingly with the means of doing an immeasurable amount of good; for no one can estimate the good which might enter into the life of a single man who is thus disposed, as witness the man Christ Jesus. In the things of this world, the men who have accomplished most have lived according to this principle of seizing opportunities. If you study carefully the lives of men who have done the most considerable and numerous works, such as Calvin, Luther, Bossuet, you will see that they did them just as they presented themselves on their way; and that they were men called by circumstances, almost imperceptibly, to achieve their works. For example, Bossuet was led by the requirements of the Dauphin's education to compose his best works; Calvin and Luther did their best work as circumstances demanded: while, on the other hand, ordinary men who do little are those who do not know how to seize and profit by passing opportunities. They might perhaps have been able to do as much as those who did great things, but they lacked the true art of seizing the opportunity. And this is the Christian art, of having the eyes always turned towards the Lord, and of thus taking each task as He presents it to us, and, when that is finished, going on to another. It is wonderful what can be accomplished in this way, by simply following the path that the Lord opens up before each one of us.

Third, we must go about our work methodically, and never leave to chance the employment of the time God gives us. I was saying a few days ago that we should not make plans for ourselves; but I am not contradicting myself by saying that we must work methodically, provided that the method is undertaken in the Lord. To do what God gives us to do, there must be method and order. Thus it is desirable to have regular hours for getting up and for work;

to be as punctual as possible at meal-times and in all our various occupations. Life then becomes much more simple and easy to cope with; it will be like a well-ordered framework in which the Lord has only to act. The men who have done most have been those who have known how to regulate their lives calmly and steadily, above all if they have been able to add to this firm discipline a liveliness of mind and a warmth of heart which do not always go with this spirit of method and order, but which, when combined with it, enable a man to do the most astonishing things. It is said that the philosopher Kant would sometimes amuse himself by calling his servant to witness that for forty years he had risen every day at four in the morning. Just think what a man can do who gets up at four every morning! Besides, think of the power of method, whatever time a man gets up. From the fact alone that I have a fixed hour for rising, how much more time will I not have to consecrate to the Lord, for the simple reason of having fixed the hour in prayer before God, taking into account Christian wisdom and prudence; while on the contrary, if I rise haphazardly, the hour will be determined by the impulse of the moment, that is to say, by various circumstances over which I might otherwise have triumphed—by my idleness, by my desire for "a little more sleep, a little folding of the hands in sleep; so shall thy poverty come as one that travelleth", and not only poverty of money, but of spirit, of labour, and of the service of God. Thus method, in a life peaceably regulated before the Lord, is a thing of the highest importance, if we would learn to accomplish much for the service of God.

And finally, not to multiply reflections, let us keep our bodies and minds in such a condition as will bring no obstacle in the way of the good use of our time and our gifts which God has given us, to employ according to His will. Sadness, unevenness of temper, the seduction of self-will, the seeking of our own interests, the desire of human glory are so many obstacles that surround and harass us unceasingly, and over which we must seek to triumph.

Then, let us not neglect the body. Bad health, and bodily weakness are often a great obstacle to the accomplishment of our work for God. We must accept what God sends; but it is our duty before God to take all necessary exercise and precautions to strengthen and preserve even our bodies for His service and glory. This thought uplifts and sanctifies everything. Many men would have accomplished much more than they did for the glory of God, if they had not given themselves up to an activity which was more pious than thoughtful, and which wore them out while they were quite young. Moreover, those who die prematurely should ask themselves whether they have not to reproach themselves for neglecting certain precautions, simple and easy though difficult to persevere in, which would have allowed them to work longer in the service of God. But above all, let us be careful to strengthen the mind and the soul, and to avoid all that would impede the work God will accomplish in us and by us.

My friends, none of us knows how long God may still leave us here; but we do know the time He has already given us, and the reproaches we deserve for the use we have made of it. Let us lay hold of what is still before us, whether strong or weak, sick or in good health, living or dying. We have a Saviour every moment of whose time was given up to obedience to God: let us follow in His footsteps to glory, by way of the cross, and at the end we shall hear that loving voice saying: "Well done, good and faithful servant; thou hast been faithful over a few things, I will make thee ruler over many things".

XVII

A DYING MAN'S REGRETS

4. PRAYER

[3 February 1896]

MY dear friends in Christ, among the matters concerning which the Christian who is near his end feels regret there is surely none which he would desire more to reform, if he were restored, than prayer. What is prayer, really and practically, for most Christians—I mean believing and praying Christians? A few moments in the morning given to meditation, a few moments at night, sometimes long, sometimes short, sometimes very short; then also, the heart lifted up to God in extraordinary circumstances which make us feel a special need for drawing near to Him—these are the meagre proportions to which the habits of many Christians are reduced, or people who call themselves Christians. So how little do the greater number know of the fruits of prayer, so often promised in Scripture! Where can they be, those mighty fruits of sanctification, which make the soul triumph over all temptations, as Jesus did in the wilderness, and which make us more than conquerors through Him who loved us? And where are those fruits of consolation which spread a sweet and profound joy through the soul, capable of prevailing over all earthly affliction, so that even in bitterness and anguish, whether of heart or of mind, it can still rejoice with that perfect joy which Jesus, as he was about to die, bequeathed to His disciples who were to lead a life of daily dying? And where are those fruits of deliverance in which the soul obtains from God all that it asks, whether it says with Jesus: "I know that thou hearest me always"; or whether, unable to rise so high, it says with David: "Thou art wont to hear me"? Let us be sincere and recognise that, between the promises which the Scripture makes to prayer and the benefits that we receive from it, there is such a great distance, that more than once our feeble faith has been troubled, perhaps for a moment shaken, and we have said to ourselves, "Is that all?" No! that is not all that was promised; but we have not done all that was commanded. Ah! my friends, prayer as I have just depicted it for you from life is quite different from prayer as Scripture presents it to us, and to which it makes all the promises.

What is prayer *not*, according to the Scripture? I was saying the other day that Holy Scripture, the Word of God, is Heaven speaking on earth; I would say, to pursue this image, that prayer according to Scripture is Heaven received within us by the Holy Spirit. Without the Word, prayer is null and void, having no nourishment; without prayer, the Word is powerless and does not penetrate into the heart. But when the truths of Heaven, with which the Scripture is full, are received and assimilated into the substance of our soul by prayer, and penetrate into the very depths of our inner man, then we know that prayer brings Heaven within us with all its wealth, the Holy Spirit and all His grace, God and all His promises. Prayer is the key which God has placed within our hands to put us in touch with the unseen world: by it everything is available to us, and without it nothing. I say, the key that God has placed in our hands, for there is another which He has kept in His own, and which He deigns to use sometimes to open up to us the unseen world, when we have neglected to open it for ourselves to enter into communion with Him and into line with His divine action, according to that which is written: "We are labourers together with God". Thus God, in striking down Saul on the Damascus road and raising him up a new man, opened Heaven to him, when Saul, far from seeking Him, sought the disciples of Christ to torture them and destroy them. But there we have acts of grace which we must not count upon; indeed, the more we count upon them, the less they will be granted to us. Without doubt, if one pondered well upon it, even behind these special acts of grace, the sincerity of the soul in seeking God would be found. This Saul of Tarsus, who went about persecuting the Name of Jesus in His followers, had nevertheless a sincere heart, which sought for God and enquired for the truth; and perhaps from the moment when St. Stephen had prayed for those who put him to death, who knows but that the spark of a new life had begun to enter into the soul of Saul? Be that as it may, God's normal way is to bestow His blessings in answer to prayer, and to wait for prayer before granting them. "The Lord", says Isaiah, "waits that he may be gracious". What does He wait for? He waits until you have cried to Him. And in Jeremiah: "When ye shall go and pray unto me, I will hearken unto you. . . . And ye shall find me, when ye shall search for me with all your heart". The same is true of us. It is by prayer that we can obtain everything, and it is to true prayer, such as the Scripture depicts to us, that all the promises are made.

Also, my friends, prayer is the distinctive mark of the mighty servants of the Lord. With all their considerable differences, they all have this in common: they are men who pray much and men who pray earnestly. Take the prayers of a Jacob: he wrestled with the Lord for a whole night, until he prevailed even with the Lord Himself, who allowed him thus to prevail in order to exercise the faith of His servant. Take the prayers of a Moses, the founder of Israel, of a Samuel, the reformer of Israel, of whom Jeremiah says at the beginning of his fifteenth chapter, to emphasise that God was resolved to withhold a certain blessing: "Though Moses and Samuel stood before me, yet my mind could not be toward this people". Let us try to substitute our own name for that of Moses or Samuel: when such or such a one among us has prayed, it will not be granted. What a blow! How humiliating!

How unreasonable! Then take the prayers of a David. In the Psalms are recorded prayers which not only sustained him, but, like a hundred and fifty pillars, have supported the people of God from generation to generation and will support them until the end of the world.

Take the prayers of King Jehoshaphat, who overthrew by prayer alone the combined armies of the Moabites, the Ammonites and the inhabitants of Mount Seir; and of King Hezekiah, his great-grandson and imitator, who by prayer alone called down the avenging power of God to exterminate an army of a hundred and eighty-five thousand men, who were only waiting for a chance to destroy Jerusalem and rase it to the ground. Take the prayers of a Nehemiah and an Ezra, to restore and to reform their people, following the example of Moses and Samuel; the one by raising their spiritual state and observance of the law, the other by rebuilding the walls of Jerusalem and re-establishing its civil affairs.

Then consider the prayers of Jesus, "the author and finisher of our faith", who, though He was Jesus the Son of God, prayed, spending whole nights in prayer and did nothing but by prayer. By prayer He chose His band of apostles; by prayer He sustained them; by prayer He triumphed over the devil in the wilderness, in Gethsemane, and on Golgotha; by prayer He accomplished the whole work of our redemption, being enabled to endure unspeakable sufferings, of which the most excruciating of our sufferings is but a pale reflection. Then, following Jesus, we see beginning again the series of men of prayer. A Paul, what a colossus of prayer! Prayer is the spring and the soul of all his work. Paul is Paul above all by prayer. Consider the prayers of a St. Augustine, the prayers of a Calvin, of a Luther who, at the time when he was appearing before the Diet of Worms, spent three of the best hours of the day crying to God in a loud voice, not knowing that his faithful friend Dietrich was eavesdropping and recording those prayers of fire for the good of the Church.*

Consider the prayers of a Pascal, who, stricken at such a young age by such cruel, unrelenting sufferings, was enabled to surmount them with a steadfastness and a piety which we find deeply and indelibly marked in those prayers of his, so beautiful and so strong, which have been preserved. Consider the prayers of all the saints of all times: prayer was their faith, their life, their resource, their work.

O my friends! I do not know if you are as deeply humiliated as I am by these memories. For myself, I cannot express just to what extent I am humbled as I recall what my own prayers have been compared to what they ought to have been, what they could have been. We surely would be in our own humble sphere of action what those men have been in the history of the Scriptures and of the Church, if we knew how to pray as they prayed, and if instead of saying theirs was a special privilege which God gave them, we could say: "Lord, teach me to pray!" Ah! if my life were restored to me, I would, with the help of God and

*This is what Dietrich wrote to Melancthon (Schreiben an Ph. Melancthon, Walch, Teil XVI, p.2139), in speaking of Luther's visit to Coburg, during the Diet of Augsburg: "I cannot admire enough his steadfastness, his joy, his faith and hope in these desolate days. He strengthens himself each day in his convictions by a constant application to the Word of God. Not a day passes but he reserves *three hours at least* for prayer out of the portion of the day which is most suitable for work. One day I had the privilege of overhearing him pray. Great God! what a spirit, what a faith in his words! He prays with all the devotion of a man before God, but with all the confidence of a child speaking to his father. "I know" said he, " that Thou art our good God and our Father; that is why I am persuaded that Thou wilt exterminate those who persecute Thy children. If Thou dost not do it, the danger is to Thee as much as to us. This cause is Thine: what we have done, we could not have done otherwise. It is for Thee, merciful Father, to protect us." When I heard him from a distance praying these words with a clear voice, my heart burned with joy within me, because I was hearing him speak to God with altogether as much fervour as liberty; above all he supported himself so firmly upon the promises in the Psalms, that he seemed fully assured that nothing he asked could fail to be accomplished."

watching against myself, give much more time to prayer than I have done, and rely upon it more than upon work, which, though it is our duty not to neglect it, has no strength unless supported and quickened by prayer. I would, above all, breathe out in my prayers that unction and fervour of the Holy Spirit which is not learnt in a day, but is the fruit of a long and often painful apprenticeship.

O my friends! you are full of life, you whose career seems not yet to have come near to its end—although we know nothing of this and I might live longer than you—seize this opportunity and redeem it; begin new habits of prayer. Bring to your prayer not only a spirit of fervour, but combine with it a spirit of order and method which will increase its power, as it will increase the power of all things human, and will even promote the divine power itself; that order and method of which Jesus Christ has given us an example in the Lord's Prayer, which is the model prayer.

Finally, pray God to guide you, and depart from this place, with this prayer filling your minds: "Lord, teach me to pray!" I will apply myself to it with you, however short the time may be: God is not concerned about the brevity of the time, but with the uprightness of the heart. Let us all together, with one heart and one mind, humbled by the slackness of our prayers, form a holy resolution to know definitely by experience what His promises really are, that we may reap the full benefit of them in that unseen world, with which prayer alone through the Word of God brings us into relationship. For that unseen world is now near to some and far from others—farther than they think or wish, but, be that as it may, in ten, twenty, fifty or even a hundred years—it makes no difference—for in the twinkling of an eye it will open for all those who have placed all their hope in Jesus Christ crucified and risen from the dead.

This is my earnest prayer for you, and if the Lord calls me to Himself, it is the heritage that I would leave to each one of you, commencing with my beloved family! Amen.

XVIII

A DYING MAN'S REGRETS

5. PRE-OCCUPATION WITH PETTY INTERESTS

[10 February 1856]

MY dear friends, once again you give me a token of your brotherly love by sharing with me in the Lord's love-feast. Now, one of the matters which would trouble the soul of a man who is facing death, if he were not comforted in this as in everything else by the free grace of God in Jesus Christ, is the memory of that part of his life which has been wasted, if nothing worse, in petty interests, when he ought to have been occupied with those great interests which alone ought to be constantly before the eyes of a Christian. That is why I wish to call your attention for a moment to the great evil there is in the Christian being pre-occupied with petty things.

Let me explain at the outset that we must not confuse pre-occupation with petty interests with attention to little things. We are called upon by God to occupy ourselves with a host of little things, and it is chiefly of such things that life is made up. The manner in which we fulfil our smaller duties is quite as true a measure, often more true, of our piety than the way we do the great, because in the little we have only God, ourselves and our family as witnesses, whereas in accomplishing great things we are placed in a sort of theatre, where our pride is sometimes only too well gratified to see us established in the public eye. Besides, nothing is great or small in itself: it only becomes so by the spirit we bring to it. In God's sight, what we call little is as important as that which we call greatest, and what we call great is as insignificant as that which we call least, since God is infinite and eternal. A faithful servant who takes affectionate care of the child committed to her charge by her mistress, for the love of God, does something very great in the sight of God, which will receive its due reward; and a statesman who aspires, just for his own sake, to be renowned for wisdom or eloquence does something very little in the sight of God, which may bring more shame upon him in Heaven than glory upon earth. What matters therefore is that in all that we do we bring a large and lofty mind, always looking to God and doing all things as before Him and eternity; so that, having God always in our hearts, we should always have Him in our words and our works, and there would be nothing merely petty, earthly, or transitory in the whole of our life.

The example of God Himself will serve to make clear what I have just been saying. God makes no difference in the care He bestows between the little things and the great. He constructs a blade of grass or a snowflake with as much care as He regulates the proportions, the relative positions and the movements of the stars; and, whether He makes a grain of sand or plants a Mont Blanc, He does all as God, that is, with perfect care. But this God, who regards nothing as too small to merit His attention, has always in view, in His lesser works as much as in His greater, eternity, His kingdom and His glory. As He Himself says: "The Lord has made all things for his glory". And there is absolutely nothing in all the works of God, whether moral, or even physical, to which He does not apply the immense weight of an infinite regard and eternal concern. It is the same with Jesus—God made visible. Not only does He not neglect the poor little children who are brought to Him and whom the apostles regard as beneath Him to bless, but He does not overlook even the fragments of the loaves and fishes, and He desires nothing to be lost, when only a moment before, He had shown that by a word, and even without a word, He could multiply the loaves and fishes at will! And this is the same Jesus who accomplished the greatest works, in His incarnation, His redemption, His passion, His resurrection and in His glorious ascension. But He does all these things in the same spirit: and whether He becomes incarnate, or redeems us, or suffers for us, or rises from the dead, or ascends into Heaven, whether He stops to bless those little children, or to gather up the fragments of bread and fish, or to speak even the smallest word of comfort to an afflicted soul, or to offer a glass of cold water to one who is thirsty, He has always, in every one of His actions, God, eternity, and the glory of His Father in view; and it is in this way that Jesus Christ appears to us in all His works, with His head always in Heaven, though His feet are on the earth, and saying: "He who is in heaven", when referring to Himself. As everything in His soul is great, so also are all His works and thoughts.

Well then, my dear friends, that is the example set before us; and it is thus that we should walk, pre-occupied not with the petty interests of earth, and still less with its covetousness and its sins, but with God, with His glory, His love and the work of Jesus Christ for the glory of God and for the salvation of men, as well as for our own.

Made in the image and likeness of God, we should be His followers, and in the smallest concerns, as well as in the greatest, be always dominated by the thought of God and eternity. Whatever the Christian does or says ought always to be great in the sight of God, who weighs true greatness. Painters represent the saints with a halo; but the Scripture does not do that, except in the case of one Old Testament saint: certainly it does this in quite an exceptional way. The saints wear their halo within themselves, and shed it abroad wherever they go; and the Christian should give such an impression of himself that wherever you meet him, in the street, in the drawing-room, at table, in prison, or at the height of success, you always have the feeling that here is a man who seeks God, who is concerned with advancing the great interests of humanity, who considers that it is not worth living for anything else but to glorify God and who makes all his advantages and setbacks work together to that end; a man who is ready to leave this earth as soon as his work here is done, and who, like his Master, goes about doing good. Oh! how holy, and how happy such a Christian would be; free from covetousness, envy, anxiety, and all that troubles the soul, always walking with God! How he would honour the Gospel, and victoriously put to silence the gainsayers! How many souls he would lead to his Saviour, by the humble brightness of a holy life, more even than by the most powerful words!

But where are these Christians? O God, where are they? How much easier it would be to find sincere men—I mean true Christians—who if they came to die would commit their souls into the Lord's hands, and at heart are waiting upon Him, yet who let themselves be distracted by and pre-occupied with petty interests—the love of money, a thirst for human glory, jealousy of a rival, a passionate desire for personal success, an ambition for things outside the way which God has marked out for them! They are hindered by impatience with hardships, by a repugnance for humiliation and the cross; they experience sharp indignation over a word, perhaps a word misinterpreted, or in an insignificant little happening which will afterwards, perhaps even in an hour or so, leave no trace! O God! how few consistent Christians there are! It is because of this, my friends, that the Gospel is compromised by those who profess it, and it is said of them so often, that, after all, they seek what others seek, and what troubles others troubles them equally!

Thus the Gospel is harmed by the very ones who seek in it their peace and their salvation, and who ought to be employing all they have of life and strength to glorify it, by walking with head high, their head in Heaven like Jesus, with their feet upon the ground, but breathing the atmosphere of Heaven and drawing from there the spring of all their actions, the strength of all their life.

My friends, if you knew how, when you see death at close quarters, all these illusions melt away, how that which is small really appears small, how only that which is great in the sight of God appears great, how one regrets not having lived more for God, as Jesus lived, and how, if one had to begin all over again, one would lead a more serious life, more full of Jesus Christ, of His Word and His example—if you only knew!—you would at this very moment put your hand to the work, you would beseech God to make your conduct answer more closely to your convictions and your faith; you would succeed in this, as so many others have succeeded, because they cried to God and sincerely *desired* it before God. And this little handful of children of God assembled in this room, around this bed of sickness and in all probability of death, these Christians, with all their weaknesses and infirmities, would do more for the advancement of the kingdom of God and the good of humanity than a dense crowd furnished with every possible gift; and they would do things so much the greater because all thought of vainglory would henceforth be banished far from their hearts.

This is my desire for you and my ardent prayer, and it is also the prayer which I beseech you to make to God for me, so that during the time which is left to me, whatever it is, I shall think only of living for the glory of God and for the good of my fellow-men, and this will be to live at the same time for my own eternal joy! Amen.

XIX

JESUS CHRIST

[17 February 1856]

AS we reflect on what we have just done in remembering what God has given us in His beloved Son, we would gladly either remain silent or add to this solemn service only some words of adoration and thankfulness. But since the Saviour calls upon us also to glorify His Word and testify to its truth, and because, in certain situations, opportunities for doing this are so rare, I will continue to expound the truth to you as it is in my heart, relying upon the help of God and waiting for the day when the Lord will close my mouth and tell me: "Enough now; you have spoken enough; go now to rest from your labours in the bosom of your Saviour".

You know how I love to speak to you here on what I call "A dying Christian's regrets", the views of a Christian, who believes he is near his end, on the use he has made of his life, on how he would use it if it were extended, and what he would like to see his brethren do who still have their lives to live. But I feel that I am also called in my peculiar circumstances and especially in the dark and troubled times in which we live, to tell of the conclusions to which my experience as a Christian and pastor in my infirmity have led me; so that when God calls me, the convictions with which I fall asleep and rest may be well known, and there may be no doubt of any kind in the heart of my friends, my brethren, or the Church, as to what at this moment constitutes the assurance of my soul, and what I hope, in the goodness of God, will do so more and more.

There is one thing of prime importance which I will not

stop to consider at this moment, because we have recently considered it at length. I know my little congregation changes, but I cannot do other than follow a certain order in the thoughts which I pass on to you. The first consideration is that of sin. The first point is to have a clear and profound view of our sinful state before God: not only by the conviction that we have sinned against His holy law, but because we have begun to form an estimate of the enormity of sin, the terror of the judgements of God, and the depth of the abyss from which we had to be rescued. Once we are convinced of this bitterness of sin and, left without extenuation, excuse or explanation, are constrained to say: "Against thee only have I sinned", the Gospel in its entirety will be summed up for us, my dear friends, as it is at this moment for me, in one single word, or rather in a single name: *Jesus Christ*! As St. Paul said: "I determined not to know any thing among you, save Jesus Christ and him crucified".

Who is Jesus Christ? What is He? What idea do you have of Him? How do you answer His question: "Whom sayest thou that I am?" That is the basis and the beginning of our faith. (O God! strengthen my heart and my mouth to give Thee glory in my affliction! . . .)

When we think of Jesus Christ, we consider Him first as man; but we soon discover that He is no ordinary man. We find there a boundless charity, a goodness always ready to come to our aid, and a power always capable of delivering us; a master and a deliverer who heals the ills of the body to show that He can heal those of the soul, even the most secret and deepest miseries; a holiness without spot, the holiness of God Himself brought down to earth. In a word, we have here, in a human body and a human mind, divine perfection of truth, strength, goodness and freedom from sin, which no man ever possessed or imagined. And this attracts us to Him as one who, we instinctively know, alone has the power to grant us every deliverance we need.

But soon, on reading the Scripture and hearing Him

speak, this mystery begins to be solved; but by another mystery still more profound. We learn that our Lord Jesus Christ—for such is the man whom we have just been considering—born by a supernatural birth, is not only Son of Man, but at the same time Son of God: Son of Man, that is to say, *Man*; Son of God, that is to say, *God*. He has a virtue, a power, a holiness and goodness all divine, because He is God; He is the express image of His person and the brightness of His glory and "in him dwelleth all the fulness of the Godhead bodily". This is the mystery of godliness, God manifest in the flesh, God being able to say to His disciples, as we have just now heard it read: "He that hath seen me hath seen the Father".

My dear friends, it is my deep and growing conviction, and that of all faithful people from the beginning to the end; prophets as far as it was given them to discern, patriarchs, apostles, witnesses, martyrs, fathers (the faithful Church fathers), reformers, servants and handmaids of the Lord in every age; that here, properly speaking, is the key-stone of the Gospel edifice and the basis of the whole Gospel. From this point flow out all the infinite number of paths which diverge toward all the deeps of faith and obedience to which we may be called; so that the Christian life in its entirety rests so much on this foundation, Jesus Christ, God manifest in the flesh, that, short of this, not only is Jesus Christ dethroned, but also God Himself. The living God lives no longer; we are given a god of the deists, a god of the pantheists, a god of the rationalists—who is only a lifeless god, and has never saved, or sanctified, or consoled anyone, because the true God is the one who reveals Himself to us, and not only reveals Himself, but gives Himself to us in Jesus Christ; for, as someone has so aptly said: "In creation God shows us His hand, but in redemption He gives us His heart".

Jesus Christ God, and yet Jesus Christ man, really and truly man, truly and fully God, seems to many to be a speculative rather than a practical doctrine (O God!

strengthen my feeble voice and languishing soul! . . .); but it is not so; indeed, far from being a speculative doctrine, it is the very foundation of practical Christian living. Therefore St. Paul, while calling it a mystery, calls it the *mystery of godliness*: "Great is the mystery of godliness". Outside of that there is no Christian life, Christian holiness, Christian comfort, Christian power or Christian death. It is the basis of everything else, and the grace of the Lord Jesus poured into our hearts is our only strength as well as our only hope.

For this reason I want you to know and I confess that I see in Jesus Christ my God, before whom I prostrate myself with Thomas, saying to Him: "My Lord and my God!" and concerning whom I testify with St. John: "This is the true God and eternal life": or with St. Paul: "He is God over all things, blessed for evermore"! I honour Him as I honour the Father; and I know that the Father, so jealous of His glory, far from being jealous of the glory I give to Jesus Christ approves of it, as glory given to Himself, because He desires all to "honour the Son as they honour the Father"! And I endeavour to live in the fellowship of Jesus Christ, in the peace of Jesus Christ, praying to Him, looking to Him, speaking to Him, listening to Him, and, in a word, giving Him day and night a continuous stream of testimonies, which would be idolatry if He were not God, and if He were not God in the highest and most unique sense that the human spirit is capable of giving to this sublime name. Jesus Christ is *He who is*: "I am; I am the way, the truth and the life; I am that I am; Jehovah; the Lord God Almighty"—that is who Jesus Christ is: that is what He is for me. And if, in the last moments of my life, I should be prevented by sickness from bearing Him this witness, I want you to know that I bear it here and now; and I have no thought of ever going back on it, for the little faith, the little comfort, the little holiness and the little charity that I possess and that I pray God to increase, I have experienced only since, changing my first opinions,

I learnt to worship Jesus Christ as my Saviour and my God.

Being now quite sure of His Deity, I find at the same time in Jesus Christ my brother, my fellow, my friend; the one who is with me, near to me, and according to that beautiful expression in Psalm eighty-four, "my sun and my shield". My sun, that is, my salvation from afar: my shield, that is, my salvation near at hand. Between this sun of divinity and me, so many things come, the length of the road is so tremendous (and I leave it to anyone to calculate the material distance along it, although you could never measure its spiritual length) that I need the Lord near to me, like a shield covering me all over—with His heart pressed against mine, His arms constantly around me, so that I can say to Him, if I wish, in just a whisper, without anyone in the world hearing: "I am Thine, and Thou art mine; I know who Thou art, my God and my brother; and Thou knowest who I am, Thy child and Thy servant, who believes in Thee in spite of all his weaknesses, whose only complaint is that he believes so little, and who longs to go on believing in Thee till he can glorify Thee in the bitterest trials!" Jesus Christ, then, is my brother. Ah! how blessed to have God for a brother, and a brother for God! I would never even try to describe all that is involved in this profound, tender and mysterious union of God with man: that is what Jesus Christ is for me.

I can say no more about it at this moment; but you see what my thoughts concerning the Lord are, which I would be ready to confess before His judgment seat, if He called me there, knowing that He will not contradict me and that there is nothing lacking in my convictions but what is lacking in my worship and knowledge, and that I am infinitely behind in the expressions of love and adoration which I owe Him.

My friends, that is what Jesus Christ has become for me; that is what God by His grace has made Him to me, using in turn a variety of means of education, example, action, books and preaching; employing these instruments with various degrees of light in different ways and thus establishing me in His grace for eternity.

I know that He was preparing me then and wanted to give me the power to bear what He is sending me today, so that this may be the crowning experience in His dealings with me (if indeed it is the crowning; we still cannot say definitely). And I solemnly charge you to question yourselves and see if Jesus Christ is for you what He is for the universal faithful Church, what He is, I repeat, for the patriarchs, the prophets, the apostles, the martyrs, the fathers, the reformers, and for all the saints in every age; what He is according to His Word, according to His own declarations and the testimony of the Father. Rest when you have done this, but not before; for no one should rest until he has learned to rest at the foot of the cross of his Saviour God, even though he might be blown there by the winds and storms of life, and fall exhausted at that place which he will never again want to leave!

XX
THE SCRIPTURES
[24 February 1856]

THOSE who have been present at some of these meetings know that I like above all in these few words which I address to you, my dear friends in Christ, who give me such a great token of your love, to go over the memories of a Christian who believes he is ready to appear before God, and then also to gather up in His presence and communicate to you the main results of his study of the Word of God, and the convictions in which he wishes to finish his course and die. Having from this point of view expounded the conclusions to which I have come concerning sin and the person of the Lord Jesus Christ, today I will go on to speak for a short time on His Word.

I declare as before the judgment seat of Jesus Christ, at which I expect to appear before long, that all my studies and researches, whether in Scripture, in Church history, or in my own heart, and all the discussions which have arisen during these last years upon the inspiration and divine authority of the Word of God, that all these, during the triple period of my ministry,* have, though in ways that the wisdom of God has varied, served only to confirm me in the unshakable conviction that, when the Scripture speaks, it is God who speaks; that when it proclaims His will, the way of salvation, the great doctrines of sin, of grace, of the Father, of the Son and of the Holy Spirit, what it says to us is no less true and sure than if the heavens were to open above our heads at this moment, and the voice of God were

* (Three periods of about ten years each, at Lyons, at Montauban and at Paris).

to ring out as of old at Sinai, uttering the same things.

There are no limits to the confidence and the submission which we owe to the Scriptures, any more than we find limits to the truth and the faithfulness of God; so much so that, on the day, of which God alone knows the date, for which I long as a deliverance (yet without daring to hasten it), when that day comes, and I shall enter the unseen world, I do not expect to find things different there from what the Word of God has represented to me here—apart, of course, from the immense difference in the condition and state of the soul before and after death, in time and in eternity. But after all, the voice I shall hear then, which will be clothed with all power to judge, and will reign over every creature, that voice will be the same one that I hear today upon earth and I shall say: "It is exactly as God told me, and how thankful I am to Him that I did not wait to see before I believed!"

This is because the Scripture is the divine expression of truths and ideas which form the very basis of invisible and eternal things. It is like a letter which God has written from the unseen world to His children who are still detained in the visible world, so that through faith in God they may learn, here and now, how they stand and what they must do in consequence to save their souls. Those who believe God will save them, but those who do not believe God, how can they save them? The Scripture is, therefore, the Word of God in the highest and at the same time the simplest and most popular sense of that word. It is the only rule of faith and life; a rule to which all others must be subject: all the meetings there are in the world, for committees, for conference, prayer or study, have no value whatever except in so far as they are subordinated and subject to the sovereign, infallible and unchangeable authority of the Word of God. The testimony I bear to it here is the same as that which has been borne not only by Moses, David, St. Paul, St. John, Augustine, Chrysostom, and all the saints in all ages, but it is also the testimony of God Himself and of Jesus Christ, who gives to the Word of God the same glory as He receives from it.

We are also permitted to appeal to observation and experience, provided this is done with a humble diffidence; and the result is mercifully the confirmation of all this testimony. For never was it given to any man, or company of men to compose a book, be it ever so short, which equals Holy Scripture, and is capable of producing the same effects of comfort, sanctification, or conversion; never will it be given to any man or company of men to do this, unless the Holy Spirit leads them in the same special way in which He led the apostles and prophets. It is not a question of personal holiness, since this holiness which we have just recognised in the Scripture is no less present in the words of St. Paul than in those of Jesus Christ Himself: it is a question of divine direction. This divine direction appears still more clearly when you consider that this book was written in an entirely historical order and that, although spread over a span of nearly two thousand years, it has, on every point, teaching which is consecutive and consistent with itself. The Bible is a book on its own, which no other ever did or ever could equal, and it is supreme over all the systems, all the uncertainties and all the questions which occupy or disturb humanity.

But, to start a new train of thought, hardly have I for my part sanctioned the title "Word of God", which the Bible has received from God Himself and from Jesus Christ, than I find on closer examination that it is full of man. It contains so many marks of humanity; and for a moment I might have felt a sort of fright, as if I had gone too far in the testimony I have just borne to it.

I recognise indeed in the writers of this book such a marked individuality of character and style that if one were to discover today some book which had, in error, been left out of the canon (which is impossible), any man, however little versed in the Holy Scriptures, would be able to tell immediately if it was by Jeremiah, or Isaiah, or Peter, or John, or Paul; so great is the difference between these writers, and so clearly has each one stamped his character on everything he has written. I find in them many things which the writers of this book could have said without the special help of the Spirit of God (e.g. 2 Tim. 4.13, etc.); and, as God does not perform unnecessary miracles, we see that in such instances the mind of man has its part in the composition of the Word of God. What is more, I also find in it certain traits which remind us of human weakness, as when St. Paul seeks to call to his remembrance, without venturing to trust it, the number of persons he baptised at Corinth; but he is not troubled about it; "for", as he says, "Christ sent me not to baptise, but to preach the gospel" (1 Cor. 1.14-17, etc.).

It was evidently intended by God that on every page of this book which we call the Word of God we should recognise at the same time the word of man. But if anyone who does not pause to think is alarmed by this, he will soon be reassured and on the contrary will see in what is human in the composition of the Scriptures a token of blessing, light and spirituality. For how could it be avoided? It could not be otherwise, unless the Bible had been dictated word for word, without the influence of personal character or historical events. Let us take an extreme example, which I quote with deep reverence. When God places words of reproof against an unfaithful prophet into the mouth of a stupid animal, it is quite evident that His Word operates without an intermediary endowed with a will, and that the *inspiration* (for it was certainly that) is in this case all the more evident because the instrument is passive. What is there in this inspiration of a creature without reason to compare with the inspiration of an apostle, fully impregnated with his own experience and personal feelings? Such an observation, applied to all the degrees of the intermediate scale, in proportion to the activity or passivity of the instrument, would show how the inspiration gains in interest as it becomes more personal, without losing any of its authority.

Therefore, how much more beautiful, and how much more affecting the Scripture is, as it has been given to us! —given by God in the course of history, by the agency of men whose minds were led by the Holy Spirit—men like ourselves who could say: "I believed and therefore have I spoken"; men of whom, for example, it could be said: "Elijah was a man subject to like passions as we are, and he prayed earnestly that it might not rain: and it rained not on the earth by the space of three years and six months". The Word of God being given in history to men such as we are, and brought to us not by superior, invisible creatures but by men weak like ourselves, saved like ourselves, who believed first and could say: "I have believed what I exhort you to believe"—by this very fact, the Bible has a liveliness, a freshness, a power that touches our heart much more deeply, and forms between the heart and this Word a familiarity and, as it were, a secret friendship, which makes the most solemn of all books at the same time the most tender and most dear: this shows a deep knowledge of the human heart, and is one of the most precious beauties of the Word of God.

Thus the Bible, from having been composed by mere men, who had to fight constantly against sin as they were writing it and to depend personally on the faith they proclaimed, is not only no less the Word of God for that, but it is all the more divine the more human it is; that is to say, that the power and presence of the Spirit of God and His influence upon our souls are the more felt in that God used instruments to write it in whom His Spirit alone could make effective that power and that supernatural light which made of them chosen vessels to carry the truth to the ends of the world. It is for this reason that Holy Scripture wins its way into the very depth of our hearts; and, while it instructs us on behalf of God, at the same time it instructs us through men—combining at one and the same time all the conditions capable of moving, enlightening and converting to God, of drawing men out of the darkness of this age and accomplishing everything in us all.

There is, my dear friends—and this is my last thought—a contrast, or rather a comparison, which for the Christian serves at the same time to clear up and confirm what I was just saying; it is the view we were taking last Sunday, and which the Scripture gives us everywhere, of Jesus Christ uniting in Himself the divine and human natures in a way so marvellous that we cannot explain it, but which is nevertheless the foundation and consolation of our faith.

Last Sunday we began by considering Jesus in His human perfection, after which we beheld Him in His divinity. Suppose we had reversed the order and spoken first about the divine nature of Jesus Christ and the obligation we are under to worship Him as God Himself, and that afterwards we had for the first time reflected in this way: "But Jesus Christ is a man, capable of suffering, and of dying"—a certain fear might have entered into our soul, as if we had attributed too much divinity to Him. But, as we saw in that same address last Sunday, the Scripture everywhere makes plain to us that this perfect divinity is allied in Him with perfect humanity, and the one enhances the value of the other, without in any way compromising the reality of either. It reveals to us that the more He is God the more is He man, and that the more He is man the more is He God. For at what time is Jesus Christ most clearly man? Is it not in the temptation in the wilderness, in the anguish of Gethsemane, and in the frightful agony of the cross? And are not those also the times when He is most clearly God, as conqueror of the tempter, overcoming pain and triumphing over the cross by the power of the Spirit of God who dwells in Him, not by measure as in us, but without measure as in the only begotten Son of the Father?

In a similar way, this goes also for the Word of God: it is the Word of God, His true, eternal Word; and at the same time it is the word of man, where men see the spirit of man shining and the heart of man beating. And it is for that reason that one can say that it is all the more divine the more it is human, because it is precisely during moments when you see most clearly, as for example in St. Paul and St. John, the fight of faith, the persevering struggle against sin, that you see also most clearly how divine is the light which is shed forth in their souls, enabling them first of all to struggle for themselves, and then to shed this light with a divine power over the whole world.

How admirable this comparison between Jesus Christ and the Holy Scripture seems to me! Besides, it is an analogy which, you may well believe, did not come out of my own head, but one which is provided for me by the Word of God itself. For anyone who knows that it does not "speak in vain", it will suffice to call to mind a quite astonishing thing: the Scriptures sometimes give the same name to Jesus Christ as to Holy Scripture; they call them both *the Word of God*. One of them, Jesus Christ, is the living Word of God, the personal manifestation of His invisible perfections in the midst of humanity; the other, Scripture, is the written Word of God, the verbal manifestation of those same invisible perfections, given through language. They are inseparable for us: for Jesus Christ is only revealed to us by the Scripture, and the Scripture is only given to us in order to reveal Jesus Christ to us. In this way Scripture is the written Word of God, as Jesus Christ is the living Word of God. Those who support their arguments against the divinity of the Scripture by referring to its human character reason like those who argue from the human personality of Jesus to refuse Him the title of God, not understanding that the divine and human natures are united in the person of Jesus Christ, as the human word and divine word are united in the Scriptures. It is no more surprising that the Scripture, although the Word of God, should at the same time bear so many marks of humanity, than that Jesus Christ, although God, should be man. As to the manner in which the two natures in the one case, and the two voices in the other, are combined, that is the very foundation on which faith rests in this matter, a profound mystery; but as St. Paul says a "mystery of godliness" which fills our soul with joy and hope.

Yes, the Scripture is the only way by which we may come to a knowledge of Jesus Christ without danger of error, as Jesus Christ is the only way by which we may come to know the Father. Yes, if you want to save your souls, you must believe in the Word of God; you must submit to the Word of God; you must not seek anything in yourselves, whatever fine name you may give it—reason, intelligence, sentiment, conscience—to dominate, judge and control the Word of God; there is no question of controlling it, only of being controlled by it. The greatest of all the servants of God are those who bow before this Word, the St. Pauls, the Davids, the Luthers, the Calvins, zealous of humiliating themselves before it, even to the dust, and, if they could, even lower.

May it reign without a rival, this Word of my Saviour-God, to which I am so glad to be able again to bear testimony, "before I depart and am no more"—until the curtain of eternal life, which we can only half-open here below, is drawn aside completely for us in the pure and serene light above!

XXI

THE HOLY SPIRIT

[2 March 1856]

WHAT a blessing we have, my dearly beloved, if we rightly understand it, as we receive this bread and wine which the Lord Himself gives us, present although absent, and all the more present, being absent, than if He were actually present: "This is my body which is broken for you, this my blood which is shed for you." From now on we are called to do His work by close union with the Lord, and by possession of His body and blood. It is in His broken body and in His shed blood that we are called to suffer all the anguish and all the pains of the flesh; and, renewed by the Holy Spirit in Him who calls us to eternal communion with Him by this present visible communion, we have for the work of Jesus the strength of Jesus, the grace of Jesus, and the divine nature of which we have been made partakers in Jesus by the promises of faith.

But we are, alas! people of little faith! What a spectacle we would present to the world if we were people of great faith, a faith capable of exciting, like that of the centurion, the admiration or amazement of the Lord Himself!—a faith which, in laying hold of Jesus Christ, could lay hold of the eternal life in Him, and all the treasures of grace laid up in this merciful Saviour!

A few days ago, my dear friends, we were occupied in considering the thoughts in which the Christian would rest his soul when he arrived at that moment to which we made allusion, and, coming to the end of his career, he would say to the Saviour in his own small way: "I have finished the work which thou gavest me to do." (He *could* say this if he had been faithful in his own small way.) We were considering, I say, the power and truth of that Word by which the Lord has revealed Himself to us, and by which He feeds our souls day by day, so that it is to us, as it were, a perpetual fellowship in which we live by the life of Jesus Christ and accomplish the work of Jesus Christ. Let us not forget, and let us learn, whether from the declarations of God's Word, or from the humiliating experiences of our own life, that this Word, omnipotent and wholly divine, which caused Job to cry: "Oh! how strong are the words of the Lord!"; this Word has no strength except as it is applied to our hearts by that Spirit who caused it to be written in a book, who worked in the heart of an Isaiah and a Jeremiah, of a St. Paul and a St. John, and who, having chosen them as instruments, led them to give the eternal truth to all generations, without danger of error. This Word must be written again in our hearts, and, as it were, fastened there by the same Spirit, without whom it will just be dead and ineffective.

We might read the Holy Scriptures over and over again for years without receiving any real blessing from them, and we should be astonished to see them so powerless and with so little verification in our experience, if the Holy Spirit did not explain and apply them to us by coming to dwell in us.

Now the same Spirit who applies and explains to us the Word of God is also the one who does everything else in us. The work of the Father who has saved us freely, the work of the Son who has redeemed us by His blood, are vain without the work of the Holy Spirit, who opens our hearts to believe in the Father and in the Son and put into practice these words of life. Man—the heart of man—is exhibited to us by Scripture, in which everything is great, infinite and eternal, as a theatre which attracts the attention of the holy angels and of the Lord Himself, where a continual battle is waged between the powers of Hell and the powers of Heaven, which is but a renewal of the great battle which was waged by the same powers, inwardly and outwardly, in the life of our Lord Jesus Christ: and in which He gained complete victory and has made us in our turn more than conquerors through Him that loved us. Thus we are either the slaves and beneficiaries of the spirit of darkness, or the slaves, the happy slaves and the rich beneficiaries of the Spirit of light and life. And it is for us to choose the one by unbelief or the other by faith, for it is written: "I have set before you good and evil, choose. . . ."

Yet there is this difference, well worthy of the mercy of God. However ingenious the spirit of Satan is to seek an entrance through every door of our hearts, he is nevertheless incapable of uniting himself wholly with our spirits and making us one with himself; but the Spirit of God deigns to enter within us and so to unite Himself with us, that we become temples of the Holy Spirit. And being filled with the Spirit of Jesus Christ, we are made capable of doing the works which He did, and of doing in a sense even greater, as He Himself said when he gave the promise of the Holy Spirit: "He that believeth in me, the works that I do shall he do also, and greater works than these shall he do . . ."; so much so that Jesus declares to His disciples that because of the Spirit whom they are to expect from Him, it is better for them that He should go away: "It is expedient for you that I go away".

O my Saviour! how many times I have wished to have Thee near to me, like Peter and John, to be able to approach Thee, to converse with Thee and to consult Thee! But Thou Thyself hast declared that there is a gift so precious that in order to secure it, it is better for me that Thou shouldst go away, and this gift Thou hast granted me by the Holy Spirit. Where are those who know and appreciate the gift of the Holy Spirit? All one can say is, may God grant to those who are faithful in the Church today the grace to see how little they have appreciated and possessed this creator Spirit who is none other than God Himself coming to dwell in us and to make all things new, this

Spirit to whom nothing is impossible. Happy is he who believes and does not doubt! If I have to overcome a dreadful temptation, it is not I who must overcome it, but the Spirit of God in me whom I call upon by prayer. If I have to endure pains unbearable to the flesh, it is not I who must endure them, but the Spirit of God in me whom I call upon by prayer. If I have to put on the spirit of love, which is so contrary to our natural selfishness, it is not I who have to exercise that power of love, but the Spirit of God in me whom I call upon by prayer—and the same with everything else; so that to doubt that we can by the Holy Spirit accomplish the work to which we are called, we must first doubt that God is faithful to His promises, and consequently that He has the necessary power to fulfil them.

"O my friends", said one dying Christian, "even on our best days we only have our eyes half open." And I apply that word particularly to the virtue and the power of the Holy Spirit: for if we had our eyes wide open to see and appreciate Him, would there be among us so much groaning and complaining, and would we not always be seen to be filled with the power of union with Christ for accomplishing our work?

My friends, look at the place which the Holy Spirit occupies in the Scriptures, which He occupies in the promises of Jesus Christ to His apostles, the transition He effects from the Gospels to the Acts, and the immense change which he produces in the apostles themselves, in order to show all disciples in all generations what He is able to do in every age. The Holy Spirit is the great promise of the New Testament; He it is who crowns it all. Chosen by the Father, redeemed by the Son, if we come to be filled with the Holy Spirit and to live the life of the Spirit, then and only then are we put in possession of our inheritance, awaiting the time when we shall receive, in a better world and under a more peaceful sky, the fulness of this inheritance, loosed from all the infirmities of the flesh and of earth; when we shall be so completely the temples of the Holy Spirit, that even our bodies will be called glorious and spiritual bodies.

Fall soon, body of dust and of sin! to give place to that glorious body, that spiritual body, in which we shall perform the will of God as perfectly as Jesus Christ Himself, and we shall know by the light of the Holy Spirit all the gifts of the Holy Spirit and all His graces; we shall know them to enjoy them, and above all learn to love as we have been loved.

XXII

EVERYTHING IS IN JESUS CHRIST

[9 March 1856]

1 *Cor.* 2 : 1-10

IN recalling with you, my dear friends, the convictions which my experience of life and of the gospel ministry and my study of the Word of God have strengthened, I said last Sunday: "Everything is by the Holy Spirit." Today let us go on to say this: "Everything is in Jesus Christ." We are inclined sometimes to imagine Jesus Christ as having only opened the door of Heaven to us, and then, so to speak, as having abandoned us to walk through it by ourselves. But that is indeed a narrow view of what the Lord has done and of what He is for us; and surely St. Paul had higher thoughts when he wrote: "I determined not to know any thing among you, save Jesus Christ and him crucified." For him, God was summed up entirely in Jesus Christ and Jesus Christ was summed up entirely in His cross. And he wrote in another place: "He is made unto us wisdom, righteousness, sanctification and redemption," by which we see that Jesus Christ has not been given to us only to wipe out our sins by His blood shed once and for all, but that He has been given to us, once we are reconciled to God by this precious blood, to lead us, to sanctify us, to fill us with wisdom, and to accomplish all in all. And again he wrote: "In him dwelleth all the fulness of the Godhead bodily"; it is in the flesh, under a visible form, that God dwells in Christ, but He dwells there fully with all His glory and all His eternal perfections. And yet again in another profound passage, the same apostle wrote: "All things are yours, and ye are Christ's, and Christ is God's", where we see God, through an admirable and marvellous hierarchy, at the head of the whole system of eternal truth sending forth His Son and leading Him; and His Son, in turn, calling us and adopting us to Him, in order that, in the Name of His Son, we should rule over all things, and that we should possess the entire universe as the right of members of Him to whom the whole universe is subject. "All things are yours", is the first degree; "and ye are Christ's", the second degree; "and Christ is God's", the third, or rather the first and supreme degree, to which all the rest are connected, and on which all the rest depend.

How far we are now in our thinking from those who represent Jesus Christ as having accomplished only one act, the principal act of our salvation! Jesus Christ is the God to man, as Pascal has so well put it in a passage where he develops, in a profoundly Christian manner, the place which Jesus Christ occupies between God and us; He is the God who gave Himself to us; He gave Himself entirely; and when we possess Jesus Christ by true faith, we possess nothing less than God Himself, and, in Him, eternal life: "He that hath the Son hath life . . . God hath given to us eternal life, and this life is in his Son."

Therefore, whatever need we are concerned with satisfying in our souls and in our entire existence, earthly or eternal, we find satisfaction in Jesus Christ. Is it first of all a matter of having our sins blotted out? He has blotted them out with His blood. There is only one thing in the world which can blot out sins: it is not our penances, or our repentance; it is not our alms or our good works; it is not even our prayers; it is the blood of Jesus Christ: "the blood of Jesus Christ cleanseth us from all sin." Every sin covered by the blood of Jesus Christ is forever annihilated before God. God Himself sees them no more: I could employ even stronger expressions without wandering away from Scripture. "God himself will seek them," says a prophet, "and will no longer find them . . . he hath cast our sins behind his back," so as not to think of them any more. "He hath cast them into the depth of the sea"; and looking at us in Christ, He sees us without sin, as Christ Himself, who "was made sin for us, that we might be made the righteousness of God in him."

Do we need to be comforted in our sufferings? We go to Jesus Christ; He suffered like us, more than us, infinitely more than we can suffer, infinitely more than we can conceive of anyone suffering; all our sufferings are only like a little stream flowing from the flood of His infinite suffering; just as from His cross flows all mercy and all consolation. Therefore it is to the Man of Sorrows that we go, to find consolation and peace, knowing that He knows what weakness is, knowing that in drawing near to Him we shall not only find relief from our pains, but we shall see in them a true blessing, and that our bitterest afflictions will in the end prove to be His most signal blessings.

Do we need light and wisdom, strength to resist sin? Whatever we need, whether in this life or the next, everything is in Christ: having Christ we have all things, but without Him we have absolutely nothing. That is why the apostle Paul says, in this marvellous passage which I was just quoting to you: "All things are yours, and ye are Christ's, and Christ is God's". All things are yours, if you are Christ's, who is God's. No-one will challenge the relationship which God has to Christ; no-one will be able to challenge that which Christ has to us, if we are true Christians. So then, what may we conclude from this?—that all things are ours.

Am I poor? All the fortunes in this world are mine; for they are Christ's, who is God's, and He could easily give me, with Him and through Him, all the fortunes of this world, if it were for my good. If instead of riches He gives me poverty, then it is because that is best for me, and what God has chosen. The whole world, with all its glories and all its power, belongs to me, for they belong to my Father, who will give me them tomorrow and who could give me them today if it was for my good; for He disposes of them as He pleases.

Am I ill? Health is mine, strength is mine, well-being is mine, and the full enjoyment of all the good things of life is mine. For all these are Christ's, who is God's and who disposes of them as He pleases. To whom would He vouchsafe them, if not to me, His child? If, then, he refuses them to me today, for a fleeting moment which passes like a weaver's shuttle, He has His reasons for doing so; it is because, in this suffering and bitterness, He has hidden blessings which are worth more to me than health, which is so precious, and well-being, which is so sweet. He never deprives me of any good thing, except to grant me something better: that is my consolation, all in His love.

Do I need wisdom and enlightenment? Well, though I were ignorant all my life, through not having the opportunity of cultivating my faculties in the world, I would still be a wise man in Christ. Knowing Christ, I am more enlightened and more illuminated by the things of God than the man of the world who spends a whole life-time poring over his books; for I know that light, uncreated and eternal, which he does not know: the light which God Himself rejoices in, and by which I am being led unerringly through all the darkness and obscurity of life. I challenge you to find anything of which I cannot say: "This belongs to my Father and therefore to me; if He denies it me today, He will give it me tomorrow; I trust in His love". All is mine if I am Christ's.

Notice also that St. Paul says in the chapter which we read at the beginning: "I determined not to know any thing among you save Jesus Christ, and him crucified". O my friends, let us not be so ungrateful as to forget that it is under the cross and by the cross that Jesus Christ has obtained and merited for us this immense happiness which I am trying to describe, though I realise that I am not succeeding even in catching a glimpse, or conceiving anything of it. It is by the shedding of His blood, by His unimaginable sufferings that He has accomplished everything for us. His love is the source of our deliverance and of our complete redemption: what a Saviour!

This is where we began, and this is where we must end. We come to His cross and we sit down beneath it. We want nothing in the world to tear us away from this place; we want to live there and to die there. Dear friends, soon all the scenes of this world will have passed away. We have tribulation in the world, but be of good courage: Jesus Christ has overcome the world. The strong man has been bound by a stronger than he; and here we are now in the presence of Christ, who has redeemed us with His blood, and who waits to crown us with glory and felicity.

Do you not want His glory? do you not want His love? Know Him as He is. Embrace Him wholly by a sincere faith, so that you may realise these admirable words of the apostle, upon which we have meditated for a short time. May you be happy in life, and happier still in death; and may this life, which is so sad for the men of the world, be for you an existence in which light and peace always increase, until the day of Christ, to whom be given praise, honour and glory, and, above all, the homage of our hearts, and if it be possible, a love answering His!

XXIII

THE TRINITY

[16 March 1856]

Romans 8 : 12-17

HOLY Scripture is wise, even in its silence. You woul look in vain therein for the word *Trinity*, to express th doctrine concerning which I have it on my heart, if Go gives me strength, to speak a few words to you. Why Because this word *the Trinity* would present to our mind the idea of something speculative, while the biblica doctrine, which human theology later and very appro priately called by the name of "Trinity", is most practica and most tender, because it is the very expression of tha love which is in God, whether in His relations wit humanity, or whether in the inner relationship which Go has with Himself.

The origin of our salvation is in the love of God. "W love him, because he first loved us; God is love," and th love was made known to us in the work of our salvation yet not just as it saves us, but as it existed from all eternit in the bosom of God, and constituted His eternal felicit before it brought about ours and that of all His faithfu creatures. If we wish to appreciate fully the way in whic God's love acts towards His poor lost creatures, in order t give them the eternal life which they had forfeited by thei works, we have only to follow quite simply the historic order in which God has given us His revelations, and ha inspired His apostles to write the Scriptures, after havin done the same with His prophets. Thus we find first th God of the Old Testament, then the God of the Gospel and then the God of the Epistles and of Gospel Prophec

We learn already in the Old Testament what should b

sufficient to fill our hearts with joy (O my God! display Thy strength in my infirmity! . .)—we do indeed learn there what should be sufficient to fill our hearts with joy: namely, that unworthy as we are of His love, God has nevertheless loved us. We deserved to be condemned a thousand times over, and if anyone is not convinced of this, he has only to read the prophets again, Ezekiel in particular. They are all full of this terrible doctrine of the judgment of God which the Israelites drew upon themselves by their wicked works, but which they merited no more than the rest of mankind, of whom their history is, as it were, a mirror. God, however, instead of declaring Himself against us, has declared Himself on our side; and we find that where we would expect to see the treasures of His wrath, we see the treasures of His mercy. The Almighty God, who has created the heavens and the earth, the author of the visible and the invisible world, is altogether *for us*; He asks only to save us; and whoever will accept God's thoughts, confessing his sins and submitting himself to His grace, will possess eternal life, as if he had never sinned; or rather, he will possess it as having sinned, but as having been reconciled, and possessing a realisation of the mercy of God. This is how God is revealed to us in the Old Testament, so that, bearing away the heavy burden of divine wrath, divine love pervades everywhere. The same prophets who announce terrible judgments cannot long sustain this language, and they always end with words of mercy. You will find this in a remarkable way in the prophet Micah, who, in a few brief pages, develops with wonderful fulness the scheme of condemnation, of prophecy, and of salvation, in which he finally rests.

Then come the Gospels, foretold by the prophets. God now goes a step further: He draws near to us, not content with declaring to us, as from a distance, that He is for us; but He comes to live with us as one of us; Son of Man, taken from among men, though He is the Son of God. And having been for us, He is now *with us,* close to us, as a friend and a brother, with whom, as the fifty-fifth Psalm expresses it, we can "take sweet counsel together." Then God shews Himself to us under a more tender and a more reassuring aspect than in the Old Testament, above all when this friend and brother brings to a climax the doctrine of divine justice and divine mercy, as He dies for us on the cross, there blotting out our sins. But whilst this tender relationship is displayed between God and us, another relationship is displayed in the bosom of God Himself, for we learn that the one who redeems us is the Son of Him who desires to save us; and that there is, between God as He is revealed in the Old Testament and God as He appears in the Gospels, the touching relationship of a father to his son; a relationship which, in God, we cannot know in all its depth, but which we can at least understand to be at once mysterious and unspeakably tender.

And notice that neither of these relationships can hold without the other, and that we shall never understand what God is for us in Jesus Christ, unless we can see something of what Jesus Christ is for God—all the more because there is something here which we should not allow to escape us. We cannot understand the spirit of love in all its fulness save as the spirit of sacrifice. Now, in God, it seems there cannot be sacrifice; for how could one take a single moment from His eternal felicity? Yet we see here that, in the person of His Son, the Lord of lords gives us an example of sacrifice; for the one who is the Son of the Father is at the same time the "Man of Sorrows"; and that where "the fulness of the Godhead dwelleth bodily," here the unspeakable immensity of suffering of which human nature is capable—but of which it is capable only in this union with the Deity—is revealed to our amazed and grateful gaze. For do you not see that this profoundly moving doctrine disappears completely, unless the Son is one with the Father; and all that motivates our tender thankfulness for the Lord Jesus Christ depends on this, that He is truly Son of God, that is God; as He is Son of Man, that is man?

Then come the Epistles and Gospel Prophecy; and how do they open? By the descent of the Holy Spirit, who founds the Church as He is poured out upon her. This is the third and the last step, for one could not conceive any further step which God could take toward His poor fallen creatures. He was with us, and now He comes to make His dwelling *in us,* and to make Himself so one with us, that these poor bodies of ours, born in the dust and become slaves to sin, are made the temples of His Spirit—God's home, in which He is pleased to dwell! The Holy Spirit, that is to say God, comes in order to give Himself to us; after having been *for us* in the Old Testament, and *with us* in the Gospels, this is the last all-surpassing step of divine love, which cannot be satisfied until He becomes one with us, "He in us, and we in Him." And, here again, we do well to notice, my dear friends, that all the power of this life-giving doctrine disappears, if the Holy Spirit, instead of being God Himself, were nothing but an emanation from God, an action of God, a gift of God. For then it would only be a case of reminding us of what we already know abundantly, from the Old Testament and from the Gospels, concerning the grace and power which God can and will communicate to us; whilst the Holy Spirit, as He is revealed to us in the Epistles and in the latter part of the New Testament, and in the promises of Jesus Christ to His disciples, being God Himself, is the power of God which strengthens us, the peace of God which comforts us, the holiness of God which liberates us from evil, the life of God which beats in our hearts!

Oh! who could measure and comprehend the immensity of this advance from the last chapter of the Gospel to the first chapter of Acts, so as to appreciate fully this wonderful sweep of revelation and divine gifts in the three parts of the Holy Scriptures which we have just been examining—alas! so rapidly for such a subject, though too lengthily for the little bodily strength of the one who is speaking to you! A wonderful view indeed, which I can only outline to you!

The relation of the Father, the Son and the Holy Spirit to man corresponds to a relationship in God between the Father, the Son and the Holy Spirit; and the love which is poured out to save us is the expression of that love which has dwelt eternally in the bosom of God. Ah! the doctrine then becomes for us so touching and profound! There we find the basis of the Gospel, and those who reject it as a speculative and purely theological doctrine have therefore never understood the least thing about it; it is the strength of our hearts, it is the joy of our souls, it is the life of our life, it is the very foundation of revealed truth.

I am obliged to stop now and leave to your meditations the things which I would have added further; and I limit myself as I close to reminding you of a word which I have often quoted in the pulpit, but which some of you who are here may never have heard, which admirably sums up the whole of this doctrine. A Church father used to say: "In the Old Testament we have *God for us*, in the Gospels *God with us,* and in the Acts and Epistles *God in us.*"

May this God, for you, with you and in you, the Father, the Son and the Holy Spirit, be your God, as He is mine, in life and in death: this I pray from the depths of a heart which is devoted to you in Jesus Christ!

XXIV

THE RESURRECTION

[Easter Day, 23 March 1856]

Ephesians 2 : 1-10

IT is written: "Faith is the substance of things hoped for, the evidence of things not seen"; that is to say, it has the double virtue of making future things present, and invisible things visible. Now if there were one fact in which this double virtue of faith might be found active and, as it were, incorporated—adding to the power of faith the clearness of reality—would it not be the very foundation of all our knowledge and the most substantial support of our hope? This fact is the resurrection of our Lord Jesus Christ.

Scripture begins by so uniting the Christian with his Saviour by faith, that what happens to Him happens to us, and the history of Christ is reproduced inwardly, but essentially, in each one of His children. If He dies, we die; if He rises again, we rise also; if He ascends into heaven, we also ascend; it is by this means that we are saved, because we are made one with Christ by faith, and as we are not allowed to look for Him anywhere but in life and eternal glory, we are obliged to look for ourselves there also, being one with Him by faith. But note that Jesus Christ, after living and dying before the eyes of men, also rises from the dead before their eyes, and shows Himself to men after His resurrection. In other words, the resurrection of Jesus Christ, which belongs to us like everything else, becomes a visible event, which makes visible our own resurrection, though it was invisible. You remember those heretics of whom Saint Paul speaks, who said that the resurrection was already past, considering it as a purely spiritual thing: they are in flagrant opposition to the doctrine of the Gospel, which makes of our Saviour's resurrection, and also of that which we ourselves must enjoy after Him and with Him, a real, material, corporeal fact, and which in the resurrection of our Saviour displays our own resurrection as already visible to the eye. What an immense blessing and privilege, for the Christian to contemplate his own resurrection in Jesus Christ visibly raised from the dead, making that which seems, and in a sense which is, invisible become visible in his Saviour! It is thus raised high above, not only the doubts, but even the very difficulties of faith, and becomes an obvious, palpable fact which we find in Jesus Christ, and which we can seize hold of and apply to ourselves.

Then, at the same time—for, in the state I am in, I can only indicate my thoughts—the resurrection of the Lord Jesus Christ changes a future event into a present and even a past event. If He were not risen from the dead, we would always contemplate the resurrection as something to come, and hence as always presenting something obscure and intangible, although God's promises would still be certain in themselves. But here God has joined to His promise a historical fact. Jesus Christ is risen, and He has been seen; and our resurrection, which is united to the Lord's and depends on it, thus itself becomes a historical fact, a present fact, a past fact! That is why Saint Paul says: "We are already raised from the dead." Thus, by His resurrection, our Saviour has made our salvation visible, instead of invisible; present, instead of just future: what more could we ask? Only the Christian can thus possess a firm assurance of his reconciliation with God and of his eternal felicity, because for him, things invisible have passed into the domain of things visible and present, and he enjoys contemplating them in some measure with his eyes and grasping hold of things already present.

Furthermore, my dear friends, you may notice that wherever the resurrection of our Saviour is put into the shade, the assurance of our salvation is also. Thus in the Church of Rome, where attention is constantly drawn to the death of our Saviour Jesus Christ and not to His resurrection, where the principal and essential ceremony of the Church, the Mass, is the celebration of the death of Jesus Christ, there is no assurance of salvation. Indeed, they even have scruples against being sure of one's salvation, as if it were a sort of pride, and certain passages of Scripture are twisted to make them mean that one is never permitted to be sure of one's salvation; which means that there is never any peace, any firm hope for the Christian. Unhappily there are many Protestants who are no better off, and who cannot rejoice in the assurance of their salvation; that is because they do not think of Jesus Christ as raised from the dead, and now living and interceding between God and us, and of the things which take place between God and our souls as living, present, and historic. But the Christian who is enlightened about the resurrection of our Saviour enjoys the assurance of his salvation; he is as sure of it as he is sure that Jesus Christ is risen, and to make him doubt his eternal hope, one would have to begin by making him doubt that Jesus Christ was raised from the dead. That is why the day which we are celebrating is the greatest day of the Christian year, and the event which we remember today is not just *an event* of the kingdom of Heaven, but *the event* of the kingdom of Heaven; it was the resurrection of our Saviour that the apostles applied themselves essentially to teach.

And as for us, my friends, let us seize hold of that resurrection, let us live with the risen Christ, and we shall enjoy this precious privilege. But at the same time let us not forget at what price this resurrection was bought, and what path Jesus Christ had to tread, so that our hearts might enjoy the happiness of that assurance only with a feeling of profound thankfulness and love for Him to whom we owe it.

Accept these few words in the love of the Lord, as I

address them to you—this is all that I am capable of saying—and let us each one apply ourselves to enter into their meaning before Him in the silence of prayer, and in the study of the Word of God, at the feet of Jesus Christ risen, and in the love of Jesus Christ crucified! Amen.

XXV

GOD IS LOVE

[30 March 1856]

Psalm 100

It was I who asked our friend to read us this Psalm, dear friends. I must use my remaining strength only in thinking about the love of God. God has loved us: that is the whole teaching of the Gospel. Let us love God: therein lies all its morality. Hardly knowing whether I will be able to make myself heard, I gather up the little strength that I have to invoke with you the eternal and infinite love of God:

O God, who art love, who doest nothing in us and will do nothing in us except by love, how should I thank Thee enough for sending these brethren whom love assembles round my bed of sickness and suffering and of what else Thou alone knowest! I rejoice in their love. Could anyone be given more evidence of it? Would not I be the most ungrateful of men if I was not the most thankful? That is why, O my God, I give Thee thanks; and I thank Thee still more, if it is possible, for Thy love, which has so much afflicted me, but so much sustained me, and I confess it before these who have never left me to want for anything, although I have often been lacking in faith and in patience, and am far from having attained that perfect patience to which I aspire most. But Thou hast been goodness itself; and while there remains to me one breath of life and strength, I will confess it before them. Thy goodness, Thy goodness! My God, I give Thee thanks for the freeness with which Thy goodness is manifested in freely pardoning me all my faults; me, the chief of sinners, the least of Thy children, the poorest of Thy servants—but also the one whom Thou hast loaded with blessings, and of whom Thou hast made use for the advancement of Thy kingdom even until this very hour of exceeding weakness and pain into which I am sunk this day! Oh! I give Thee thanks that Thou has given me a Saviour. Without Him, I confess, O my God, I should be irrevocably lost, and today would be in the most frightful despair. But I have a Saviour! who has saved me freely by His shed blood, and I want it to be known that I rest wholly upon this shed blood; that all my righteousnesses, all my works which have been praised, all my preaching which has been appreciated and sought after, —that all this is in my eyes only filthy rags, and that there is nothing in me capable of making me stand for one moment before the brightness of His face and the light of His holiness. But now it is not I who shall be judged: it is Christ in me, and I know, I know certainly that He will enter there, and I with Him, and that He and I are so made one, that He could never enter and leave me outside.

My God, I give Thee thanks with all these friends to whom Thou hast granted the same privilege and the same consolation, and to whom Thou hast deigned to give the Holy Spirit, as to me, to apply to their souls the free gift of eternal life through the blood of Jesus Christ. I give Thee thanks first of all for my dear family. I give Thee thanks for my brothers, my sisters, my friends, who have all been brothers and sisters to me, and who now testify by their love and by their tears, their tender sympathy, which I have not in any way merited, and of which I recognise that I am entirely unworthy, but which Thou has put in them for me, and which is such a great comfort to me.

I give Thee thanks for all things. I give Thee thanks for the consolations which Thou hast poured out upon this week; for the nomination of the Professor at Montauban, which has been such a great subject of concern and prayer for us; for the Peace-treaty signed this very day,* for which we have prayed to Thee so much because we think that

* The Peace of Paris, which formally ended the Crimean War.

peace on earth is proper to anticipate again, as it did before, the peace which comes down from above. It is true, Lord, for I will be sincere before Thee, that I am suffering much, and that my joy and my thanksgivings are indeed darkened by these sufferings and continual exhaustion. But Thou hast upheld me hitherto and I have this confidence that my prayers and those of my family and my friends will obtain for me that perfect patience.

And now, Lord, I take them all, these friends, and I commit them into Thy paternal bosom, in the Name of Jesus, by the Holy Spirit. May every single one who is in this room meet again in the eternal tabernacles, and seated at the table with Abraham, Isaac and Jacob, may we be able to remember, with unmixed joy, the day which brings us together.

Oh! My God! Sanctify us perfectly, and may all that remains of our lives be employed completely in Thy service. May Thy Spirit dwell in us, and be the soul, the life and the joy of all, and their families, and their afflicted ones. Oh! Lord, many of us have sick ones, very dear sick ones; we commend them to Thee. I bear them all on my heart before Thee. I will not name them, for fear lest in my weakness I forget one of them and give pain to someone here; but I take them all and place them at the foot of the cross of Jesus, so that Thou mayest console them and sanctify them. May Thy grace and peace be with us all, now and ever! Amen.